The **Joy** of **Adulthood**

Tom & Betty,

May you continue to discover
the keys to living a life of passion
and joy.
Conscious ness is the Key !
My Blessings —
Sylvia (Reuter)

Why would you consider reading this book and putting its principles into action? Just listen to some who have written about the difference these distinctions have made in their lives.

I began to work with Sylvia when I was sixteen years old. Now, as a college student, I realize that I already had the privilege of learning communication skills that most will never have the opportunity to learn throughout their lifetime. Having the ability to distinguish between the child, adolescent and adult behavior allows me to evaluate my actions, as well as my reactions to situations so that I may make healthier choices. I count on miracles in my life.

Lindsey McD., Age 20, Art Student.

Cancer rearranged my priorities. Then Sylvia's work gave me the tools to put those priorities into action, making my life purposeful, meaningful, joyful — and a lot more fun.

Paula S., Age 50, Writer and Mother of three.

As a middle-aged gay man, I am discovering my real potential for living after surviving decades of what I thought was being an adult. I had no idea how growing up with an abusive, alcoholic father and an overly protective mother, who is the master of codependency and manipulation, would affect every aspect of my life. I never knew happiness. I yearned for authentic intimate relationships. After just a month of working with the distinctions, I began to glow, walk tall and smile. I have been liberated from my own fear, and I courageously look forward to a bright new future.

James Y., Age 43, Critical Care Nurse.

I am more fully present as a result of being aware of the Child and the Adolescent; there is play time and there is work time. I truly can close my eyes, visualize driving down the road and recognize a passenger in the car as my Adolescent who is just flapping away about something. I now allow the Child and Adolescent me to take me back to places in the past where I was most vulnerable — to situations that remind me about my current vulnerability. The different characters of me serve each other well. My Adult embraces the Child and Adolescent to more fully create who I am, where I am going and what my purpose is today, tomorrow and in the future.

Sue G., Manager, Age 51, a Major Accounting Firm.

Sylvia's work has helped me "wake-up" and move forward. The concept of understanding the child, adolescent and adult freed me to lead a healthier life, one in which I am designing a new career and satisfying relationships.

Stephanie S., Age 46, Retired Entertainer.

On a daily basis, I have opportunities to choose the words and actions I use when I am communicating with others. Although I am still a beginner, having the ability to choose my words and actions from an adult place allows me to act and speak with integrity and consciousness...what a freedom it brings.

Rozanne C., Age 47, Computer Sales and Training Consultant.

It's a luxury to experience the adult. It's a real kind of abundance and a palpable sense of security. In a way, it's almost the beginning of life.

Morgaan S., Age 56, President, Forest Light, Inc.

Sometimes, I can stop myself mid-sentence, recognize that the adult me isn't the one playing at that moment and choose to resume control of my life with a conscious adult present. It's like directing and substituting different actresses to make sure that the best one is present on the life stage at that time. It's really fun when I choose to send in the child or the adolescent because they are skilled at things like play and adventure. Without these distinctions, my life would be less effective and much less graceful. I am truly thankful to have been given specific, useful and immediate tools for taking charge of my life whenever I notice that things are out of whack. Thanks a million.

Rachael S., Age 48, Attorney, Wife and Mother of six.

In all my years of personal growth, the most useful, life-altering tool has been the ability to call forth my Adult. I cannot imagine where I would have ended up had I not known how to make sure that my Adult was making the important life decisions.

Paula M., Age 57, Manager Customer Education Solutions,
a Health Services Computer Company.

Having a conscious adult available, one who is distinct from the child and adolescent me, allows me the opportunity to make effective choices. The distinctions and the ability to choose who will be in charge of my life have created a freedom to refrain from automatically responding from past beliefs. Miracles are abounding in my life.

Lydia S., Age 61, Advanced Practice Nurse and Therapist.

The impact of knowing the distinctions of the child, adolescent and conscious adult has been profound. It has been especially helpful when I'm in the middle of a conversation and realize that the child or adolescent me is driving the communication. I then have an opportunity to step back and consciously allow the adult to come forth. While in the midst of a divorce, and at the same time caring for my sick mother, starting a new career and handling other family crises, these distinctions, and the ability to bring forth a conscious adult have been invaluable.

Judy S., Age 55, Personal Business/Life Coach.

Understanding the Child, Adult, Adolescent archetypes outside of the traditional Transactional Analysis model has provided me a personal, creative and fun way of understanding who I am when I am speaking from a certain voice. The distinctions help me recognize and be accountable for who I am. Sylvia's model has also shown me what I can expect in response to a limited Child voice and how to actualize the Adult voice. I now know that in order to achieve optimum results, it is essential to honor my authentic and powerful Adult voice and to be who I really am, moment by moment.

Jocelyn P., Age 35, Clinical Nurse Specialist.

Knowing the sound quality and words that my child, adolescent and adult use, I can now choose to communicate from my adult. Doing so has been beneficial to my relationships in all areas of my life by providing more clarity, aliveness, integrity and freedom.

Rev. Stella K., 59, Spiritual Counselor.

I have experienced several significant life woundings, including that of being the daughter and sibling in a severely addicted family, the mother of a disabled child, a rape victim and a partner in several dysfunctional love relationships. My work with Sylvia has allowed me to confront my pain and loss and to create a future that is no longer driven by my past. I celebrate the energy and aliveness that "the kids" bring to the party, but now I choose the conscious adult me to present herself in taking care of the kids with understanding and compassion. My spirit soars with boundless freedom…it is good to be home!

Kim L., Age 50, Massage Therapist and Public Relations.

I have repeatedly suggested that Sylvia put a warning label on her work like the Surgeon General's warning label on cigarettes … such as, *"This work will be hazardous to your current way of life. Your life will never be the same."* While the end result is being free to live life at choice, the path of getting there is courageous and challenging.

Terry W., Age 52, Director of Information Services.

The Joy of Adulthood

A Crash Course in Designing the Life You Want

By Sylvia Sultenfuss, RN, MS, CS
Human Relations Consultant

Palladium Productions

2004

The Joy of Adulthood / Sylvia Sultenfuss

Copyright © 2004 By Sylvia Sultenfuss, RN, MS, CS
Palladium Press
3098 Piedmont Rd., NE, Ste. 430
Atlanta, GA 30305-2600

This publication is sold with the understanding that the author and publisher are not engaged in rendering legal, financial or other professional advice. The services of a professional should be sought for individual personal advice. The author and publisher specifically disclaim any liability that is incurred from the use or application of the contents of this book. Any names, characters or incidents are the product of the author's perception, memory and imagination. Any resemblance, if any, to real-life counterparts is entirely coincidental.

Sultenfuss, Sylvia
The Joy of Adulthood: A Crash Course in Designing the Life You Want

Cover Design: Leslie Hodges
Layout: Bookcovers.com
Copy Editor: Evelyn Still
Style Editor: Eric Shamblen

ISBN 0-97490-941-6

Dedications

To the Divine from which all my gifts and visions flow.
To my family who have never ceased in their
support and demand of me.
To my clients who trust me and know more about
who I can be than I do.
To my friends who allow me to be human and
honor me as my commitments.
To the child and adolescent beings within me who
continue to allow the adult commitment to win.

Acknowledgements

So many people have pressured me to write this book. Thank you for keeping my feet to the fire. To all whom I have held as my teachers, I am deeply grateful.

To my son, Eric, you are my light and always call me forward to learn and be a better me than before. You are the best editor I could ever have hoped for. Thanks for informing me when I found my voice, a voice I didn't know I had. To Eric's wife, Friday, thank you for loving my son and for bringing a creative business perspective to my work. You have both been computer gurus for me and are true geniuses.

Thanks to all my clients who trusted me to coach them in becoming more conscious, powerful beings. To Allie, who calls me forth to be her midwife to the next level, even after 20 years. To Carol, my first client, who demanded healing miracles and taught me that it is all possible.

Gratitude goes to all of my writing buddies who shared with vulnerability and allowed me the same: Nancy Bent, Darlene Roth, Dr. Nell Rodgers, the APA Goddesses and the Million Dollar Author group.

Thank you to Tom Bird who made it all so simple; just breathe, let go, envision and then, write. To David Thalberg from PTA, thanks for getting the simple clarity of my message and recognizing the power of the adolescent.

To my dear and treasured friends who have been the foundation from which I leap into possibilities beyond my current ability to manage, I am grateful for your grounding support: to Stella Kondo, for keeping business details handled, Berniece Mercer, for preserving my sanity at home and to Terry Willey, for providing a backdrop of life that inspires me to continue living my own principles.

To Kim Lisenbee, Debbie McDermott, Dr. Vinnie and Caryl Procita and Loraine Bates Noyes for believing in my message and bringing me into your homes so that others could experience miracles.

To my edit readers, for being wonderfully ruthless and for providing great clarity for my message; a special thank you to my sister, Mary Reuter, OSB, Tim State and Mary Mallison.

Thank you to my fine editing and design team: Evelyn Still, copy editor extraordinaire, Leslie Hodges for graphics, BookCovers.com for design and formatting and Jessica Sheridan, photographer.

Table of Contents

Introduction

One day many years ago, when I had just started my practice as a psychotherapist, I was working with a client who was threatening to kill himself after a recent breakup with his girlfriend. Sobbing, he told me how hopeless his life was, how stupid he had been to let her slip through his fingers, and how he had no intention of living life without her. Life was just too painful. His intention to die was serious, and I prayed for guidance as I listened and coached him.

I spoke with compassion for the depth of his pain. I told him that grief was appropriate, and this could be a time for healing. I suggested new possible futures for him. Each intervention on my part was met with increased wailing and defensive rationale for taking his life. "You just don't understand. Nobody can understand what she meant to me. She was my life, and now my life is over!"

I listened intently to this child's voice, and I asked the client to bring his adult-self into the room so that I could talk to him. "This is my adult. This is me…all of me!" he declared.

Continuing to acknowledge the pain of a frightened and helpless child, I repeatedly encouraged him to bring an adult-self forward who could protect this child and provide safety in this time of disruption. He cried and wailed and lashed out. I kept asking for an adult to step forward, while making distinctions that would allow him to see the hurt child that was present in the room. I pointed out that he was all curled up, feeling helpless and confused about his life. "The child cannot handle the loss you are experiencing. He has the right to have an adult present to nurture and protect him right now," I coaxed. "Will the person sitting on that couch right now be able to help you through the difficulties you are facing?"

Suddenly, the man curled up even tighter on my couch and then took a deep breath, inhaling loudly. As he exhaled, he sat up, straight and tall. "All right, I'm here now."

It was as though he had birthed himself out of the victim cocoon that had encased him. His voice possessed strength of commitment and alert attention. Without any previous coaching about the distinctions between the adult and child, this suicidal man revealed an adult-self that had been generated only as a result of his intention. I was surprised and grateful for his transformation. I began to wonder whether anyone could alter consciousness and way of being, perception and behavior, if the facets of the child and adult characters were differentiated.

From that day forward, I began to identify more about the characters in the wardrobe of human possibilities. I began to delineate aspects that were obvious to me and seemed to be unavailable to others. This man's ability to bring forth an adult-self in the midst of his fear, pain, defensiveness and resistance allowed me to see the value of bringing to consciousness the distinctions about the Child, the Adolescent, the Researcher/Observer, the grownup Adult by Default and the Conscious Adult by Choice, distinctions with which I had inherently lived without realizing their importance.

Over the last 25 years, I have worked to expand these observations and make them more available to myself and to others. This book is a result of that research.

In our human journey, our experiences and beliefs provide the backdrop for the interpretations that define our personal reality. We may have been unconscious about the decisions we made as we traveled our life's journey, but the patterns of beliefs endure powerfully and continue to affect how our lives are revealed. We can review and explore our journey from a commitment to discover, to heal and alter patterns that no longer support the person and the life that we desire. Choosing to reframe perceptions and interpretations that are inconsistent with our current vision and commitments will evoke a clear sense of authenticity.

In revealing our stories, we begin to notice decisions made, emotions inhibited and beliefs engrained that define our reality. These past-based patterns may now interfere with designing the life we envision and hope for. Decisions made at the time of a particular incident may have been appropriate and necessary for survival. They may no longer be useful in designing the life of an Adult who has an expanded perspective and understanding to bring to the situation. Revealing the defenses and decisions produced by the Child and Adolescent at a time of pain or fear can allow the Conscious Adult to reeducate, redesign and rehabilitate the patterns and emotions of the child and adolescent reality. Since we are the interpreters of our reality, it is important that we discover the hidden beliefs that are defining our perceptions. If the current reality does not seem to match our intentions, we may be able to detect a sabotaging belief that is interfering with our current desires and actions.

Consider this book as an opportunity for everyone — whether people consider themselves to be already successful in the game of life or whether they are struggling. This book offers the opportunity to bring forward a Conscious Adult at every moment, an adult who is clear about the freedom to choose and create a life that is satisfying no matter the circumstances. Every day is a new beginning. Every situation reveals more information about unconscious beliefs and automatic reactions that are programmed into our systems. The commitment to continuous learning forces us to be persistent beginners who masterfully design and continuously choose to live life as a Conscious Adult. The Conscious Adult actively engages in responsibly bringing forth exciting prospects for building new futures for humanity and for allowing the soul's destiny to sing. We do have the freedom to design and choose a new way of living life and a new way of being human.

This book is designed to engage you in your own process of exploring your life's journey. Your personal discovery of experiences that were important in defining your perceptual framework will continue to be revealed as you work through the book. Each time you read a section, you may gain more insights, revealing hidden emotions to be expressed and stories to be redefined. It is my intention that as you continue the reading, you will continue to unveil new meaning, with greater depth and subtlety, about your beliefs and their impact on your current reality. As you realize these distinctions, your freedom of choice will expand, and the opportunity for designing a conscious and joyful life will be more evident.

As you work with the concepts in this book, I invite you to hold your discoveries and insights to yourself long enough for a shift to occur. To those who share easily and readily, I invite you to keep things to yourself as you reflect on their meaning and mattering. Some withhold and are uncomfortable sharing things that are personally meaningful or insightful. To them I say: Learn to share. Discover the humanity that occurs in all of us. There is no need to learn alone. Like a cake baking in the oven, let the ingredients bake long enough to ensure that the cake is done all the way to the center but not too long that it becomes hard and difficult to chew.

The Process of Growing Up

Many times as youngsters we heard, "Just wait until you grow up. Then you'll understand why things are the way they are. Then you'll understand that you have to work to get ahead; that you have to stop all these shenanigans; that you have to be responsible and stop acting so childish." We may have promised ourselves that we would never turn out like our elder grownup models. Or we may have idolized them, wanting to turn out just like them, and worried whether we would have the stamina and persistence to do so. Either way, integrated into the process of growing up was a burden of expectation.

And grow up we did — at least in age and size. If we look closely, we may discover that we are fulfilling the futures that were predicted for us by our elders. When we reacted to their expectations, whether we rejected or embraced them, we designed Adults by Default. As children and adolescents, we may have rebelled, but still became what we resisted. Or we may have experienced the safety and predictability of the parent figures and absorbed the patterns and values with ease. Often the beliefs and cultures we were born into are integrated without notice or fanfare. Mostly they are absorbed unconsciously, noticed only when we bump into them later in life: The day I heard my mother's voice speak to my young son through my mouth, I was repulsed. How could I have become what I had promised myself I never would? Would my son rebel and resist me as I had my mother? It was a day of revelation and shock. I promised that day to listen more consciously to my voice, its tone and message.

The act of getting older has little to do with whether we have the ability to consciously design an adult who chooses the principles and directions for our lives. Much of what we do and think is driven by the past. We save our money carefully because our parents did — or because they didn't. We have children because that's what was modeled — or we don't, because it was modeled painfully. We are blind to the impact of the decisions and patterns developed by the Child and Adolescent as they went out into the world and encountered obstacles and woundings. We live life unconscious about the desires and hopes that are still held by the Child and Adolescent.

Somewhere in our grownup lives, we begin to realize we're stuck in a loop, no matter how many times we change relationships, jobs or careers, presentations or hair color. We assume that we are changing the quality of our lives along with the conditions. However, in very short order, we begin to recognize that our core issues are frightfully similar year after year. We learn how to cope. We learn how to handle stress. We take our vitamins and exercise. We diet and lose weight and gain it back again. We read self-help books and watch talk shows, listening to self-proclaimed, self-help experts for bullet-point answers to our lives. We throw problems out to our friends hoping for new answers and guidance. We receive advice that we either do not or can not act on. We learn how to survive, and we even brag about our survival tactics and stories. Even with the external signs of success, we often sense an emptiness. We sometimes wonder why we don't feel successful and don't feel a sense of satisfaction or joy about our lives. There is a nagging feeling that there may be more wonder, more pleasure and satisfaction available. The question, "Is this as good as it's going to get?" invades our normal daily activities.

If we realized that our present lives are past-driven, are influenced by the beliefs and decisions made in a different time and place, what would be our response? Do we really want the child and adolescent values and perceptions to be determining our current reality? Do we really want our lives to be dominated by the emotional reactions and unconscious expectations defined by a child and adolescent self? Do we want those perceptions to be designing our lives, our relationships, our businesses?

Imagine life if the Child and Adolescent weren't running the show. What if there was a Conscious Adult choosing the response in any conversation or situation? Perhaps we have a unique opportunity to alter how we respond, think and feel about our lives without changing any of the external circumstances. If we can identify the distinctions of the child and adolescent parts of us that are running our lives, we have the opportunity to make new and more informed choices. A Conscious Adult may be able to live in the moment, in present time instead of the past. The Adult can discern the elements of the current situation, while at the same time comprehending the automatic reactions precipitated by the past-based beliefs. It is then that conscious choice is available.

Voice Indicators

One indicator for determining which character might be engaged in any situation is the quality of our voice. Listening sensitively to our external and internal conversations opens the possibility of hearing the quality of voice, the tone and gist of the messages and sensing whether the voice is that of a Child or Adolescent. Creating an objective Researcher/Observer who can distinguish the quality of the voice and its messages is one of the first steps in discerning and making choices that are consciously designed.

What does the Observer sound like? We have all experienced the voice of an adolescent observer who is a punishing critic, the one who incessantly places a negative or defensive explanation around our decisions and behaviors. This adolescent critic voice manages behavior through shaming, humiliation and guilt. "Well, that was stupid. You should have known better," or "What did you expect?" are common accusations. "It's never enough," "I never get credit," or "It's always my responsibility," are frequent defensive reactions.

An adult Researcher/Observer is not interested in blame and credit, but in discovering the distinctions and motivations about a particular situation so that more effective decisions may occur as a result. The voice of the adult Observer is calm, interested and without judgment or justification. Often the comments are, "That's interesting. I wonder what, why and how." Through the eyes of the Adult, we begin to discern what is working or not working and what is missing in our lives. We are then able to choose new directions and principles from which to live. Conscious Adults have the freedom to choose the quality and direction of their lives.

Consciously designed adults create the quality of life they desire by living consistently with principles that matter to them. They design dreams for their future and open the doors for a life beyond the predictable. The voice of the Adult by Choice is grounded, balanced and driven by an internal passion of being. The adult voice communicates with clarity, compassion and creativity, which inhibits reactive behavior and diffuses defensiveness.

The quality and tone of the voice is a unique way of identifying whether the Child, Adolescent or Adult by Choice is speaking. If we can hear the voice distinctions and interact with the intention and the voice of the Conscious Adult, a totally new way of being is available to us. The shift in perception may seem simple, but the demand to be conscious is not easy, even when we know the impact of behaving unconsciously and reactively. The distinctions may seem obvious, but the impact of altering the way that we design ourselves as conscious adult human beings is profound.

Bringing a Conscious Adult Forward

Many of us have experienced moments when we behaved in a way that was grounding and supportive without offering judgment or advice. It is difficult to sustain that resonance of presence. It requires that in each moment we recognize that there is a choice about who will respond for us, who will interact, who will engage in the conversation. Will it be a child or an adolescent, or will it be an adult who is recognizing the voices of the kids, has relieved them of duty and is consciously choosing the response or action to take in each situation?

Whether or not we feel that our lives are successful, there is always more that we yearn for...more love, satisfaction, success, intimacy, joy, freedom and peace. When we are able to bring forth a Conscious Adult by Choice who designs and directs our choices, we are no longer dependent on the conditions in our life to determine our happiness. Each day is a new opportunity to dip into the beliefs fashioned from the past, discover whether they will support our current commitments and intentions and conceive new possibilities and actions. The process of exploring, reinterpreting and redesigning is a life-long process. If we can give ourselves permission to continuously and consciously choose to redefine our boundaries, and if we give ourselves permission to be beginners in opening the door to new possibilities, we may be successful in designing a new way of being human, a new way of living life.

Using the distinctions of the Child, Adolescent, Researcher/ Observer, Adult by Default or Adult by Choice to reveal and explore the aspects of your own thought and behavior patterns offers expanding options for choosing new possibilities for your life. The distinctions are not meant to be used to damage or define who you are or who someone else is. I ask that you use the distinctions for exploration and designing rather than for harming yourself or another. The discovery and redesigning can be a life-long process if we continue to sustain our commitment to being conscious.

The Design of Your Life

The following is a process that I have used for years to guide my clients in discovering significant elements along their life journey and in identifying the many roles of their Child and Adolescent characters that reveal themselves along the way. The intent of the process is to trigger insights that may give clues to belief patterns that are affecting your life. Allow your imagination to be alive as you follow the process and engage in the journey. I invite you to read the process and encourage you to take notes as ideas begin to emerge. Answer the questions that are presented as though you were truly engaged in the conversation. Make the process as real as you can.

The Process

Choose a place and time in which you can be quiet, relaxed and uninterrupted for about 30-40 minutes. Take some deep breaths, breathing in through the nose and filling your lungs completely, then breathing out through the mouth, pushing out every ounce of breath. Imagine the breath filling you with grace, love and light, and allow yourself to relax deeper and deeper.

Take another full breath, and imagine a time before you were born, when you existed as an energy force considering whether or not to participate in playing the game of Humanity on planet Earth. See yourself looking down on the planet Earth, the big blue marble. You see that at this particular time there is an opportunity to learn about and heal all the lessons and patterns of many lifetimes. You see that in this lifetime you can be a part of transforming what it means to be human. You decide that you want in on the game. You want to play.

There's only one problem: you don't have a piece, a physical form with which to play. In the game of Monopoly™, you use a race car, an old shoe or a top hat; in the game of Humanity, you use a body. So you go to the council of elders, the wise ones, the game referees, who distribute the pieces. They ask you to first write a life script for yourself and to get certain souls who will agree to play significant roles with you in this lifetime. Off you go to write your life script.

Next, you ask certain souls to play the game with you, to take on significant roles in your life. Some may sign on easily; others may cautiously resist. How do you enroll them? Perhaps you say, "I have chosen to learn these lessons. I ask for your help in learning them." Or perhaps you enroll them by reminding them how you served them in another lifetime, and now it is their turn to respond in kind. However you can enroll them, you do.

Then you bring the signed contracts, along with your completed life script, to the council of elders. "Please give me my piece," you plead.

"Not so fast," they reply. "Before we give you your piece, you must answer a few questions, so that we know that you have put into your script all the elements necessary for the game of Humanity."

Life lessons

First question: "What lessons did you write into your script that you are committed to learning in this lifetime?"

Looking over your script, looking over your life so far, what repetitive concerns and issues do you see? Instead of classifying them as problems, consider them as lessons that you are committed to resolving. Look at conversations around love, relationship, communication, intimacy, trust, power, productivity, shame and fear. What are your repetitive patterns of concern and upsets that you can now claim as lessons?

Barriers in your life

Second question: "What hurdles, barriers and bumps in the road did you place along your life path?"

These obstacles seem to demand that you learn and master your life lessons. Look at the people, places, situations and incidents that have occurred over your life journey. See how they affected you, changed you and cloaked you with defenses. How have you learned to jump and clear those hurdles? Have you avoided them or confronted them as challenges to overcome? How did you heal yourself when you experienced the bumps and falls? Did you truly heal and embrace the hurt, or did you develop protective defenses so that you would feel no pain?

Destiny contributions

Third question: "What contributions do you intend to make in this lifetime? Why play the game at all? What difference do you want to make?"

Listen for the whispers of dreams and desires that may still call you. Listen for the futures that your Child and Adolescent envisioned for themselves. Were they fulfilled? Will they be? Do they still hold a life force of wishing and hoping? Can they be completed or released so that new dreams of your Adult can occur?

What will you do to make a difference, to support others, to bring new ideas forward or to bring something to fruition? Begin to see the always-present pulls and pushes in your life, the drives that motivate you. Feel your passion and pleasure when you are engaged in those things that are important to you.

What now may begin to emerge is the recognition of how perfect the training cycle of life on the Humanity game board is; that in order to make your contributions, you must learn the lessons and confront the hurdles along the way. Or perhaps another way to look at the training is that by focusing on making the contributions, you will automatically confront your lessons and hurdles.

Your gifts and talents

The fourth and final question: "What gifts, talents and powers do you want from us, the elders, to bring to this life?"

Again, look over your script and your life's journey. Identify those characteristics and abilities that you know and recognize. Identify those gifts that others tell you that you have, whether you claim them or not. Explore those gifts and talents that you admire in others. Are they also, perhaps, yours? Perhaps you have the gifts of intuition, sensitivity, vision and imagination. What about humor, playfulness and fun? What about integrity, authenticity, persistence, determination and the power to persuade others? Do you have innate intellectual and emotional intelligence? How about the power of language, memory and the ability to integrate and conceptualize? You decided that you wanted many of these gifts — maybe even the whole ball of wax.

"Are you sure you want all these gifts?" asks the council. "If we give you all of these gifts, you might feel a bit strange, different or unique from other human beings. You may feel lonely or isolated. Are you sure you can handle that?"

In the energy state that you are, you boldly declare, "Yes. I can handle these gifts. I need all of these gifts in order to do what I came to do, to be who I came to be."

All of this happened before you came whooshing down through the tube as an infant child into the game of Humanity, forgetting your part in co-creating your life. Look at the family and the era that you were born into. Look at the impact on your choosing those particular parents at that particular time. What influence did those particular elements have on your life? Explore the history and the decisions you made that have affected your life.

The Child You

See the Child you, five years old or younger. What was that Child like naturally — the interests, passions and personality? Look through the eyes of the Child and see what life was like. Was it a safe world for the Child? Was the Child loved, honored and respected? Was the Child listened to, heard? Did the Child have a language to communicate what it saw and felt? Was the Child supported in understanding the world it had entered?

And now, imagine that the Child turns and looks at you. What does the Child see? What does the Child think of you, of how you turned out? Let the Child know you have come back to claim it, to heal it and embrace the stories of the journey. Your intention is to validate the Child's experiences and feelings.

Tell the Child you that you are committed to loving, listening and maintaining a safe environment for healing. You say, "Imagine, Child, a place in which you would feel totally safe and creative, a place where you can be healed and express the natural magic that lives within you. Find a place in nature that you claim as your special place of safety."

Now take the Child to that safe place. "Child, it is important for you to stay here while the grownup now matures and designs an Adult by Choice." See the place of safety with as many details as you can conjure. Bring in a guardian spirit whose only job is to secure the safety of the Child. Place a protective shield around this safe place, so that nothing will intrude.

Know that the Child will stay in this safe place as long as it feels loved and secure. *The new job of the Child is to:*

1) be loved by you,

2) be safe, and

3) have fun.

If the Child does not feel loved by you, the Adult, it will go looking for love in all the wrong places. You may already have evidence for that. The Child must now be relieved of all the other jobs it has taken on, especially that of survival. It is up to the Adult to release the Child from the survival-based behaviors and to promise to take on that job for the Child if it becomes necessary.

If the Child does not feel safe, it will leap out of safety with a physical hit to the gut, the solar plexus and with a tightness of the chest. The Child will feel as though it has been deserted, abandoned and that there is no one present managing and directing the Child's life. The Child has long been the one to make sure that survival is being handled. The Child knows how to survive, but it is a survival based on feeling that it never received enough of something such as love, freedom or play.

The mantra for the Child is "I never got enough."

Taking a deep breath, now allow the Child to be cocooned in safety as it heals, rediscovers how to have fun and expresses its natural gifts and talents. Promise the Child that you will return to get to know it better, to love it and listen to it.

The Adolescent You

Take another deep breath as you bring forth the Adolescent you, the teenager. Without a conscious choice, the hormones emerged and the Adolescent evolved. See the changes in the Adolescent from the Child. What was the Adolescent like? What was the Adolescent passionate about? The Adolescent began to realize that soon, it would have to manage and direct life. It looked around at everyone else to decipher what tools, what guidance there might be for designing itself as an Adult. It observed role models and began to see all the games people play. The Adolescent made many "not that" decisions about how to do life: "I will not be like my mother. I will not be like my father. I will not work so hard. I will not be poor. I will not be fat." The Adolescent discovered few role models to emulate — most it perceived as models of what not to do. Rejecting what seemed ineffective or lacking was enough for the Adolescent. Rebelling and defining itself as anything but "that" was a natural and necessary separation of the Adolescent from the grownups around it.

In this process of testing and discerning, the Adolescent became a great actor, refusing to allow anyone to truly see what it was feeling, refusing to be vulnerable. Trying several different hats (both literal and figurative), styles and modes of being and dressing, the Adolescent experimented with how it wanted to look, behave and be perceived. In addition to becoming the actor, the Adolescent learned how to become the script writer, the director, the audience and the critic. The critic always voted "not good enough," and the Adolescent felt as though it had become an imposter that would one day be shamefully discovered.

The mantra for the Adolescent is "I am not enough."

The Adolescent designed a persona that was to carry it through life, protecting it from ever being revealed as incompetent or vulnerable, protecting it from all shame, pain and fear. Look and see what elements of your own personality have you feeling inauthentic, shallow or fragile. Now allow the Adolescent to see the current you. Have the Adolescent see how you turned out.

Tell the Adolescent that you are now committed to designing a new Adult, a conscious, spiritual Adult, an Adult by Choice. Thank the Adolescent for having produced a very competent Adult by Default and for making sure you survived this far. Remind the Adolescent that if it continues to run the show, this is as good as life will get. The Child and Adolescent have taken you as far as they can, but many dreams and yearnings are left incomplete. It will now be the Adult's job — your job — to be the script writer and the director of life, designing a life by choice. If the Adolescent continues to run the show, you will feel the drama, the weighted burden of responsibility, the suffering of the martyr-within, filled with righteous judgments, justifications and defensiveness.

Imagine that the Adolescent now passes you, the Adult, the torch of life. It will demand that the Adult be trustworthy of the job and may test you to determine whether you have what it takes, and whether you will protect the Child so the Adolescent doesn't have to any longer. You begin to realize that the Adult by Choice can not and will not exist without being conscious, and without choosing it at every moment. The grownup, unconscious adult, the grownup Adult by Default, has had a long and demanding role. Its patterns are well-defined and occur without thinking.

The mantra for the Adult by Default is "I am doing the best I can."

To open the doors to new possibilities, you must get to know the characters within — become intimate with their patterns of thinking, their voices and the automatic behaviors that have defined their identities. Know them, be compassionate with them, validate their reasons for having defended themselves in this particular way and thank them for having survived this human journey. Let them know that you, the Conscious Adult by Choice, will now take over and embrace them and their stories, while designing and casting new futures.

It is now the job of the Conscious Adult to rehabilitate, to love and to heal the Child and Adolescent within. *The new job of the Adolescent is to be the eclectic actor who functions under the direction of a competent Adult director whom it trusts.* The Conscious Adult by Choice can direct the Adolescent to expand into new untried roles, to explore many new possibilities of personalities beyond the tried and true roles that the Adolescent overuses. If the Conscious Adult by Choice is not present, the Adolescent will step in — things will go back to the way they've always been.

The Researcher/Observer You

Now, taking a deep breath, let the Adolescent be and bring into your visual memory that time when you left the nest and the supposed security of home, high school and friends. Was the departure by choice or by default? Did you leave to begin new adventures of college, travel or a job — or was it to get away from something painful? Remember the excitement and anxiety of stepping out on your own, of being in charge of your own decisions? Notice how long that feeling of self-direction lasted before there was a crash, a disillusionment, an upset that had you quickly defaulting to the defensive posturing of the Adolescent, that left you distrusting your abilities to make a different life for yourself. If the Researcher/Observer does not feel free to not know, to explore and design new options, it will defer to the Adolescent, who dislikes not knowing, fears looking stupid and will say, "I'll just fake it 'til I make it."

It is the job of the Researcher/Observer to explore and create options and bring them to the Conscious Adult by Choice for direction and decision-making. It is not the Researcher/Observer's job to be responsible for life and all that it brings. The Conscious Adult's role with the Researcher/Observer is to sustain the energy of research and exploration, to give questions to chew on without demanding a specific answer. Rather, the questions are those that open possibilities without quick closure, without singular answers. Examples might be: "What is intimacy?" "What would life be like without me judging myself and others?" "What is the possibility of being conscious all day long?" Each of these questions opens the door for endless exploration, and the responses to the questions will change daily depending on your experience and perspective. If the

Adult by Choice discovers how to ask powerful, engaging questions without demanding a "right" answer, the Researcher/Observer will greatly enrich the quality of living. The Researcher/Observer notices without voting, without judging, without shutting down the exploration with opinions. *The mantra of the Researcher/Observer is "Life is interesting."*

The Conscious Adult by Choice You

Now bring forward into your imagination the Adult you, the conscious, competent Adult that you want present to manage and direct the team of Child, Adolescent and Researcher/Observer. Remind the Adult of its responsibility to manage and direct each member of the team, making sure that each does its job — and not anyone else's job. Review their jobs. The job of the Child is to have fun and be loved by the Conscious Adult you in absolute safety. The job of the Adolescent is to be the actor, under the competent direction of the Conscious Adult. The job of the Researcher/Observer is to explore, to create options, which are brought to the Conscious Adult by Choice for decision-making and direction.

In addition to managing the members of the team, the Conscious Adult's job is to design a life of the 3-Ps: Purpose, Principles and Possibilities. Purpose: A place to come from, not to get to. *Principles:* Guiding principles that sustain and direct the quality of life, not rules and regulations, shoulds and should nots. A principle is like a weeping willow tree whose trunk is flexible, with roots that travel deep and far to sustain a water source and to hold the tree stable, even through difficult storms. *Possibilities:* Researching, exploring and creating ever-expanding, never-ending openings for life, continuously bringing forth ideas and options beyond the norm. Asking questions that open conversations for discovery without quick and simple answers is the key to sustaining a life of continuous growth and evolution of being.

The mantra of the Conscious Adult by Choice is "Anything is possible."

The Future You

And now, imagine the Future you, the person that you have hoped you could and would someday become. Let go of concentrating on what the Future you looks like, or what the Future you is doing, but rather focus on what it feels like to be in the presence of the Future you. What is its character, its sense of well-being? Feel the integrity without judgment and the intimacy without fear. Feel the freedom balanced with a trustable stability, the peacefulness along with the ability to take a stand. Feel the passion and compassion, the joy, the humor, the giggle, as though the Future you understands the joke of life.

Know that if this vision is your future, then the Future you now becomes your coach, your guide and your consultant. Imagine that you sit with it and ask for guidance — for if this is where you are going, what you will become, then the Future you must know how to get you there. Know that getting there will require that you begin to live consistently with the qualities of being there in the present time.

You have designed your new management team: The Researcher/Observer for exploration and development, The Adult by Choice as the manager and director and The Future you as the consultant.

Most of humanity is living in the reality designed by the grownup Adult by Default, one generated from the past-based beliefs and fears of the Child and Adolescent. It is critical that the Adult by Choice remembers that it does not and can not exist unless it is created at every moment, stepping forward from nothing except your word, your intention and your commitment. The Conscious Adult is only available by choice and is designed only when you say so — when you choose to bring it forward. You, the Conscious Adult, are the director of the whole team. Your role is most important.

Integrating and Aligning All the Characters

Remember now all the gifts, talents and powers that you asked for before beginning this game of Humanity, before coming to the game board of planet Earth. Imagine the gifts as a brilliant ball of light energy. Put that energy in the hands of the Child you. Notice what the Child does with the gifts. Does it play with them, explore them? Do the gifts frighten or make it feel different and strange? Does the Child hide the gifts, not knowing what to do with them? Now allow the Adult to step forward, take the gifts from the Child and inform the Child that it is relieved of its duty. It is no longer responsible for these gifts. Adult, that is now your job. Thank the Child for keeping the gifts alive. Let the Child know that you have not yet mastered being the director of life and that you are consciously designing yourself to do that with competence.

Hand the Child a magic wand and ask it to zap itself into a Child who is having fun and feels fully loved by you in absolute safety. *Bling!* See what it feels like to be that Child. When that is experienced, pop the Child into the Adolescent, get under its skin and look through its eyes. *Zwoop!* Adolescent, notice what it feels like to have this new Child inside of you. Before, you had to protect it — but this Child doesn't need your protection; it's already safe.

Step back out of the Adolescent and present it with the ball of light energy that represents all the gifts with which you came into life. Notice what the Adolescent does with the gifts. Does it reveal them to others? Does it use them to create an effective persona? Does it experiment with different personalities? Does it experiment with creativity and passion? Adult, validate the Adolescent's experience and thank it for surviving and keeping the gifts alive. Let it know that you, the Conscious Adult, will be responsible for the gifts from this moment on.

Give the Adolescent the magic wand and have it zap itself into a brilliant actor who acts under the competent direction of a Conscious Adult by Choice. *Bling!* See how that feels. And when it is ready, pop the Adolescent into the Researcher/Observer. *Zwoop!* Notice how that feels, Researcher/Observer. You now have some breathing room in which to explore and design new options with this healthy Child and Adolescent inside of you.

When you are ready, Researcher/Observer, take the magic wand and zap yourself into a brilliant explorer and designer who absolutely loves not knowing: not knowing the answers, not knowing how and why things occur, not understanding their meaning, but eager to explore everything. *Bling!* See what that feels like. Take the gifts represented in the ball of light energy and begin to explore them, to sense their impact and power, to imagine new possibilities that might be created and to feel comfortable under the guidance and direction of the Conscious Adult. And when you are ready, pop yourself forward into the Adult by Choice. *Zwoop!*

Adult, notice what it feels like to have this new team aligned inside of you. Take the magic wand and zap yourself into a competent director and manager of this team, a director who designs a life of purpose, principles and possibilities. *Bling!* Now, see what that feels like. When you are ready, pop yourself forward into the Future you, who is not so far away now as you once thought. *Zwoop!*

Notice what it feels like now to have the team aligned and working together. Sense this feeling as a rocket ship: everything is aligned and ready for a powerful takeoff. This is what you feel like when everyone — the Child, the Adolescent, the Researcher/Observer, the Conscious Adult and the Future you — is working together. Imagine yourself with this balanced force of energy as the foundation for your life, ready at any moment for the journey of living. Sense the freedom of your personal rocket ship, your powerhouse that has its destiny and power aligned, on target and on purpose.

Take a deep, full breath and allow the energy to be real. Acknowledge who you are and who you came to be. Imagine the new you living your life, driving your car, doing your job, sleeping in your bed and being in your relationships. With this new and powerful alignment, feel what it is like to be living in your body, doing your work, interacting with your family and friends. Make it as real as you can. Claim the new you with the aligned and powerful energy and allow it to be naturally expressed in your daily life.

From now on, when something is out of kilter, you can see who is running your life. Is it the Child, with its high-pitched voice? Is it the Adolescent, with its nasal, defensive voice? Or is it the Conscious Adult by Choice, with a voice that resonates from the heart to the throat? You now know that unless you create the Conscious Adult, it doesn't and won't exist. Without a created Adult, the Child and Adolescent will take over and run the show.

As you complete the visualizing of the aligned you, breathe the energy and resonance of that powerful force into and throughout your body, from the top of your head through your feet. Ground the energy with a deep, full breath, and as you blow it out, imagine the energy coming through you like lightning through a lightning rod, thrusting the energy all the way through you into the core of the planet. Bring it home! Feel and imagine that aligned energy now being grounded in you. Make it real. And when you are ready, you can bring yourself back into your current space and reality. Allow the changes to be real. Explore the distinctions you discovered for expanded clarity and power.

Getting to Know Your Child

The Child's Development and Lasting Power

In the early years, the Child is egocentric, experiencing itself as the center of the universe and one that causes the reality that occurs, whether positive or negative. The Child is learning about trust and trusting in the world around it. The Child is discovering physical boundaries and the distinctions between it and the outside world. It begins to distinguish itself as an individual entity, separate from the primary caretakers.

Initially the infant Child demands to be served by all. "If I so much as whimper, someone will come to feed me, to hold me, to change my wet clothes and to keep me warm." If whimpering no longer works, the Child cries louder or develops other soliciting behaviors such as smiling, entertaining or being very quiet. Which behavior develops depends on which one elicits the desired response from the grownups in its immediate world. Whether excited or upset, the voice of the Child resonates with a high pitch, vibrating at the top of the nose, between the eyes. Usually, the eyes of the Child are wide open and expressive, or averted when in shame.

When a Child is unable able to have its wants and needs fulfilled immediately, it learns patience; it learns to delay gratification. It also begins to feel that it has lost its power and its ability to get what it wants. The high-pitched voice now becomes one of pleading and begging. Behaviors may now include manipulation and coercion, giving the grownup caretaker whatever it thinks is necessary in hopes of receiving in return. The statement, "I love you, Mommy," may be a solicitation for missing affection. If Mommy is sad or angry, the Child readily assumes that it is the cause of the Mommy-upset, and may then become Mommy's caretaker and emotional support. Even after the Child has learned some degree of patience in getting what it wants — and some skill in manipulating others to get it — it will always want more. It is the nature of the Child's journey.

The Child may also live in denial or in resistance to the parent figures that are unable to provide what the Child wants or thinks that it needs. "I'm fine. I don't need anything or anyone," might be the message that defines this Child.

Depending on our background, we may get stuck in different phases of our journey. A woman who perceived that she had the perfect father who provided well for his family and who loved and nurtured her and her mother, demanded in therapy that I educate her husband about how to be a good husband and father. The pictures from the perceived perfect past were demanding a replay in the current marriage. The child-woman was unable to engage in her role of support of her husband and family. As long as the current reality matched her childhood memories of the perfect house, the perfect parties and the perfect vacations, she was smiling. When the finances were unable to support all of her fantasies, and when she was unwilling to participate in managing the money differently, she called on therapy to get her husband fixed.

One client described his early years living in the Midwest. Both parents were alcoholics, and at three years old he found himself responsible for himself and his two younger siblings, scrounging the house for food and warmth. In his forties, he continued to choose partners who needed him the way his siblings had. He lived in a constant state of anxiety and hyper-vigilance. He worked hard and long to make a living. His grownup relationships were short-lived and lacking in intimacy. The Child was still in charge of his life.

No matter whether it had a normal and healthy life or a frightening and depriving one, the Child always feels as though it did not get enough of something, not enough love, attention, food, sweets, clothing, toys or fun. The Child makes emotionally-based promises based on feeling as though there was not enough and it lives life consistent with that belief, even into the grownup years. If the Child was overprotected and delayed gratification was never learned, the grownup life will be filled with feelings of "not having enough," of constantly being dissatisfied with the way things are.

The feeling mantra of the Child is "I never got enough."

Discovering Your Child Characters

The Child will always live within, although it may hide or withhold itself so that it is not seen or known. It is the job of the Adult you to discover the Child with all of its gifts, powers and personas and to bring it to a healthy relationship with a Conscious Adult Director who can provide the love and safety the Child seeks.

Sometimes people say they are unable to remember anything about their childhood. If that is your comment, just imagine how long your Child has been locked away, afraid and unable to express itself. The Child went into hiding for good reason. Something left the Child feeling insecure and frightened. To rehabilitate the Child within you and to establish a trust between the Child and the Conscious Adult, it is important to set aside a time each day during which the Child is invited to step forward, to learn to trust and to be known. The Child wants to be known and claimed, but may not trust you to be its protector and advocate after years of punishing isolation. If you are patient and continue inviting the Child to step forward, it will one day reveal itself. The Child may be very cautious and stay in the shadows until it trusts you. Your commitment and attitude will be important. Interacting with the Child as a real, living part of you is critical. Establish trust with the Child by showing up consistently and keeping your promises to listen, to get to know the Child and to provide a safe, non-judgmental environment.

See the Child at its best, when its spirit is free and having fun. Acknowledge the wonder and intensity of the Child's personality and exploring nature. What are the natural gifts and talents that begin to reveal themselves? Musical expression? Athletic acumen? Sensitivity and caring for others? Intelligence? An ability to communicate? Recognize and claim these gifts. If you have photographs of you as a child, get them out and remind yourself of the joyful and painful feelings that are hidden in the memories.

Identify the critical times of upset for the Child. What decisions did the Child make during these times? How did the Child protect itself from pain? What personas and characters evolved as a result? There may be many voices that reveal themselves. Often, we feel as though we may have multiple personalities when these characters become known to us. However, with diagnosed multiple personality disorder, these characters show up spontaneously and direct their own show, often without the other characters even knowing. In a healthy grownup, there is some kind of director in charge, usually an Adolescent or Adult by Default. As you develop a Conscious Adult by Choice, there will be someone available to direct the Child, someone whom the child trusts to provide guidance and safety.

A client once sketched out some of the personalities of her Child self. There was a pathetically shy and sad Child, an outrageous, expressive one, a "bag lady" and a dramatic princess. More revealed themselves as she provided safety for them to do so. As you, the Conscious Adult, get to know the faces of your Child, you can then embrace them, heal those hidden and damaged parts and mobilize the Child's passion and natural talents to full expression. You can begin to listen for the different voices and the language to discover who is speaking and trying to run the show. You can begin to see what motivates the intrusion and choose to respond without behaving reactively.

Identify Your Personal Child Characters

Each of us has learned ways of surviving in this world. The Child used its natural gifts and talents to design a world in which it felt safe from physical pain and loss of love. As a result, a unique personality was constructed — an identity which became real enough to be accepted as "just who I am." Other people bought into this identity, agreeing to keep this construct in place. Recognizing that the Child initially designed this personality to protect itself may assist in opening the process of healing and allowing for new designs and opportunities. As you, the Conscious Adult by Choice, get to know the various aspects of your personal Child characters, you can assist the Child in healing the upset, fear and pain that motivated the development of those particular child personas. You can provide a new model of re-parenting for the Child, and teach it to trust you.

Review the following Child personalities and identify any that give clues about aspects that are familiar to you. It is important to recognize that each of us has many of these different characters revealing themselves at different times. There is never just one pattern or character that plays itself out every time there is fear or pain. You may discover and design names and descriptions of additional child characters. The character naming is never meant to place shame or humiliation on you or another.

Child Personality Characters

Wanda the Whiner feels as though her needs were never fulfilled by others and that she was unable to fulfill those needs for herself. She becomes dependent on others: "You must take care of me. I need you. I'm afraid to take care of myself. I am not capable of managing my own security."

Ronald the Responsible is overwhelmed about being responsible for everyone and everything. The result is a mixture of self-defensiveness and projection of cause onto everyone and everything else. "I had to do it. There was nobody else who could. It just happened. I didn't do anything wrong. I did the best I could. They made me do it. I have no control over it."

Patti the Pleaser is afraid of punishment, loss, abandonment and rejection. She is a "good girl," always trying to meet the expectations of others. She becomes a chameleon, changing colors based on the environment, lacking a defined identity of her own. This Child can be very quiet and observing, or gregarious and pleasing. She will maneuver to get another's approval and love.

Paul the Pathetic feels that nothing he did was ever good enough. Terrible and painful things happened that were uncontrollable. The shame of the grownups around him was dumped onto this shame-based Child, often in the form of verbal, physical and sexual abuse. He may become rule-oriented and righteous, trying to fend off any further pain or disruption.

Shirley the Saver fears that there will never be enough, and in response to that fear, she collects more food, clothing and trinkets than she could ever use. Everything has value and is important to her. Shirley is deeply sensitive to the needs of children, wanting them to have clothes and gifts. She is often collecting and giving gifts to other needy children.

Richard the Royal feels justified in demanding whatever he wants. This Child may have seldom been told "no," may never have learned that there are outcomes as a result of one's behavior, or he may feel as though he never got enough, so he now deserves everything he wants. "It is my right. I deserve it. I don't have what I want, and someone should provide it."

My Way Mattie feels deprived of having fun, and may throw seriousness and appropriateness to the wind. "I've earned it. It's my turn," are statements that justify the right to let go and ignore rules and the expectations of others.

Larry the Lone Ranger figures out early that his parents are incompetent to raise him. Perhaps the parents are unable to provide for the Child emotionally or physically. He decides to parent himself and to trust his own perceptions. He may discover that imagination and fantasy provide an outlet for fear and anger. Often this Child feels flawed and incomplete. He decides that because he is so unloved and unattended, something must be wrong with him. He may design a self-image of being special, and imagine that one day his gifts will be recognized by the entire world.

Theresa the Thinker decides that the world is just too complex to understand, so she retreats to a place of quiet observation and secrecy where no one can find her or know what she really thinks. The Child designs a secret and private world, which she understands and within which she can function safely.

Stephen the Safety Monitor realizes that his parents are incompetent in providing safety. He decides to be responsible for safety himself, and thus prepares for any possible breakdowns. He becomes hyper-vigilant and often anticipates the worst possible scenarios. Unable to take risks, he designs a repetitive, predictable life that is meant to protect him from the threats of the world.

Bart the Bully has figured out that the best defense is a good offense. He realizes that the best way to avoid pain is to eliminate the influence of those who could cause pain. He controls by being loud, demanding, aggressive and dominating. He seems to part the crowds as he passes through life.

Penelope the Peacemaker is very sensitive to conflict and disruption. She decides that life will be secure and calm if she makes sure that everyone around her is happy. She strives to make things perfect, looking to see what everyone else needs and wants. She retreats in pain if she senses failure in her attempt at peace and perfection, and will begin her quiet research again, hoping to discover the keys to keeping others happy.

Gloria the Gifted has diverse interests, talents and passions. She loves many projects and activities and moves from one to another, not wanting any one of the projects to be removed or taken away. This Child is multi-talented and can do many things well. She wants it all and finds it difficult to focus on just one thing to the exclusion of others. An eclectic, gifted Child, she may be actively engaged in many things at the same time, singing while playing with toys, having a puzzle laid out in one area while building a bridge in another, starting another project when she moves to a new room. She engages in whatever environment she is currently in and forgets the one left behind. However, when this Child returns to the previous environment, she wants all the projects to be just the way she left them. Out of sight is out of mind, so many projects will be out and visible at the same time until even the gifted Child becomes overwhelmed and needs help getting things back in order.

Summary

As these Children grow older, they become more set in maintaining life patterns. You may design names for your own Child behavior patterns. Certainly do not limit yourself to the listed names. Remember that we all have many behavior patterns that have been designed to protect us from fear and pain. Imagine who these Children become as Adolescents or as Adults by Default. It is predictable that the older they get, the more permanent become their personalities. The Child's voice is always high-pitched whether happy, excited, upset or angry. Recognizing the voice can be an indicator of who is running the show. Returning the Child to its natural way of being, its natural expression of gifts and emotions while under the guidance and direction of a competent Adult is the desired outcome. Whenever we become aware that the Child is in charge, we can choose instead to bring the Conscious Adult forward to change and redirect the energies. We cannot choose consciously without the awareness, however.

Child	
Role: To have fun, be loved, secure and safe. **Voice Indicator:** High-pitched. **Eyes:** Open, expressive, averted when in shame.	**Caution:** Beware of raw emotions; panic/pain/ rage; fight/flight behaviors and role as Victim. **Feeling Mantra:** "I never got enough."

Getting to Know Your Adolescent

Without choice, without consciousness, the human being evolves from Child to Adolescent. The hormones begin to flow freely. The body molds itself into a new form. A fiery passion emerges as the Adolescent begins to have an opinion on anything and everything. Imagination and creativity abound. Sexual energies are stirred, igniting attention to the physical body and all of its features. The teen begins to define itself in relation to the outside community and searches for group identity and acceptance.

As you remember your adolescent years, note what happened to the intensity, the passion and the drama that played itself out. Notice your own body changes and the constant comparison of yourself to others in appearance, shape, size and abilities. Notice the comparisons of intelligence, the number and quality of friends and the sense of belonging to a group. The skewed perspective can lead you to decide that you are not good enough, not important, beautiful or handsome, smart, strong or competent enough. Recognize the decisions that you made as a teenager about yourself and others that are still influencing your life today.

The Adolescent mantra is "I am not enough."

To release the Adolescent from being in charge of your life, the Adult by Choice must first step forward to be known and trusted. If the Adolescent lacks trust in the Adult, it will refuse to turn over the job it has done for so long — that of managing and acting as though everything is all right. The Adolescent has not learned to trust grownups and wonders where the Adult you has been all these years. Initially, the Adult presence can threaten the position of control the Adolescent has defined. The Adolescent may respond defensively, feeling accused of having done an insufficient job.

Being consistent, including the Adolescent in conversations and allowing it to give an opinion without having to be responsible for the outcome of the situation, are all key to establishing a healthy partnership between the Adolescent and the Adult by Choice. Get to know the Adolescent you, and let the Adolescent get to know the Adult you. Let the Adolescent know that you are new to this managing position and that the Adult is committed to designing a life based on healthy and strong principles. Educate the Adolescent about the difference between the absolute rules of their definition and the powerfully grounded, yet flexible, principles that you will lay as the foundation for your life.

Give the Adolescent a New Job

Why would the Adolescent turn over the position of being in charge just because the Adult you shows up? If you take away the job it currently has, what will it do in the future? The Adolescent feels as though it has protected you from being vulnerable. You have survived through a life script that has many ups and downs, many painful and frightening memories.

One day I realized that the Adolescent me often made herself known when she experienced some threat or concern around integrity. She sometimes felt accused or attacked for making a mistake or for upsetting someone. She would also feel tense when she sensed that someone was not being totally honest with her. Her posturing was defensive and righteous with a voice that demanded that the accuser or perpetrator be exposed and punished.

As a therapist interacting with people every day who were less than forthcoming about their fears and shameful experiences, my Adolescent voice was often vehemently present. It was as though the Adolescent was a Geiger counter for credibility, authenticity and honesty. So I decided to give the Adolescent that job — notifying the Adult me when the integrity alarm was going off. My promise as the Adult was that I would always acknowledge the Adolescent's voice as valid and that I would be responsible for managing the situation accordingly. The Adult did not agree to allow the Adolescent to direct its responses. Soon the trust between the Adolescent and Adult grew, and the loud, dominating and righteous voice grew less intrusive and reactive. Once there was a trusting relationship between them, the Adolescent was much more willing to be the actor under the Adult's direction. The Adult me became more competent and consistent, and the Adolescent trusted that she would be directed appropriately.

Discover what the Adolescent did with its gifts and talents. How did it express the given talents? How did it express passion, persistence and stamina? What fears did it confront? For what did it dream? Acknowledge the Adolescent for keeping the gifts alive, for expanding them and using them to create roles and personalities that survived all these years. Acknowledge its dreams and yearnings as valid and important. Embrace those damaged and embarrassed parts. Allow the Adolescent to have value and a voice with you, the Adult.

The Many Faces of the Adolescent

Whether upset or happy, the voice of the Adolescent resonates with a nasal tone, often sounding defensive, righteous and judgmental. Attitudes and speech patterns become absolute: "It's always this way, except when I say differently." Adolescents make fast and hard judgments about life, parents, friends and anything that might affect them. Their eyes are shifting and in motion, often confrontive or avoidant, especially in the presence of a perceived authority figure or a peer threat. They are in action, in conversation and in motion. They may burn themselves out with long hours of intensity, and then crash and sleep for hours to recuperate their strength, emerging with a fresh vitality.

Adolescents often feel indestructible: "Nothing can happen to me." They may put themselves at great risk, experimenting and exploring their limits, discovering who they really are. It is not unusual for the Adolescent to attach to a peer group that gives it permission to be alive and on fire. Finding a group that accepts it will move the Adolescent away from family norms and influences to explore new identities and ways of being.

Peer groups can be warmly accepting and safe for the expedition of adolescence. These groups might also become a source of great pain and consternation. It has been said that Adolescents can be very cruel, dumping their opinions and judgments on others, including others in their peer group. They can exclude and tease mercilessly.

Adolescents realize that soon they will be responsible for their own lives and that adulthood is just around the corner. As they look around for mentors and models, for clues about how to play the game of Humanity, they are disappointed. Other Adolescents around them are seemingly lacking in compassion and integrity as they protect themselves from revealing anything that might get them a jeer from their peers. The grownup role models appear to be suffering, burdened martyrs who complain about their lives. They work long hours and have little fun or "juice" in their lives. Most grownups appear to have lost their vitality and authenticity of being.

Adolescents make promises to themselves about how they will not be, refusing to turn out like the grownups around them. They promise that they will not be among the walking dead. They envision lives without conflict, without upset, without poverty, without long hours of work. They make promises about finding the love of their life and about being free to travel, to buy what they want when they want it. Most of these promises are made without a plan of action to ensure results. The promises themselves produce enough energy to see the Adolescent through a very confusing and often painful time. The Adolescent defines a future from a significant number of "not that" reactions, such as not turning out like my parents, not dressing like my elders, not being poor, not limiting my freedom and not being a failure. The Adult by Choice must then design the "that" for living a satisfying, successful life. So if the Adolescent does not want to be a failure, the question becomes what would it take to be a success? The Conscious Adult begins to answer those questions.

Whenever the Adolescent senses fear and panic from the Child, it looks for predictable rules and "be perfect" standards that can be put into place to dissipate the anxiety. When confronted with any challenge to its point of view or behavior or when the Adolescent feels embarrassed, humiliated or rejected, the Adolescent will justify with rationalization and justification. The Adolescent perceives the attack as being "should upon," and defensive posturing is the result. One of the most important ways of eliminating or at least minimizing the engagement of the Adolescent defensiveness is to listen for a voice tone of accusation or direction that carries with it reproach and judgment.

Often in our normal interaction, we ask "why" questions. A simple question like, "Why did you do it that way?" can automatically trigger an Adolescent reaction as it interprets the question as an accusation of poor or incompetent performance. What is often interpreted by the Adolescent is, "You didn't do it the right way." Sometimes we actually use the "should" word. "You should have done it this way," or "You needed to get it done by this afternoon." All of these examples of normal and usual speech patterns usually trigger an Adolescent defensive posturing. I have often used the mantra that I learned in a seminar many years ago: "I shall not be 'should upon', and I shall not 'should upon' anyone else including myself."

During the Adolescent time of experimentation, there is an ever-present anxiety and fear that is often cloaked in bravado and a false sense of certainty. The Adolescent locks away the Child's fears of rejection, of making a mistake, of being caught in conflict, of not being able to control events around it, so that it never appears to be vulnerable to others. The Adolescent is heavily influenced by its peers and if successful, finds some way of being accepted and included in a group identity. Adolescents are actors who try on many roles and self-images as they discover what fits them and what protects them from pain and shame. The Adolescent actor soon adds to its role of script writer, director, audience and critic. The Adolescent is left feeling as though it is an imposter who one day will be discovered and exposed as a fraud. Many of the defensive traits and patterns that run the Adolescent persona are designed to protect the inauthentic Adolescent from ever being revealed. The healthy role of the Adolescent is to be the actor under the direction of the Conscious Adult director. The additional roles of script writer and director are put in the hands of the Adult. The power of the audience and critic are relinquished into a background of unimportance.

Identify Your Personal Adolescent Characters

When you give names to identify the many characters of the Adolescent, you can begin to hear their different voices and repetitive messages. As you recognize the different characters and their roles in your life script, the Adult you can explore then being the director who determines whether a particular Adolescent character will be allowed to play on the stage of your life's drama. Without knowing and hearing the Adolescent characters, there can be no opportunity for effective directorship of the Adult. If you can't observe and know the Adolescent characters and the impact of their patterned responses, you will be unable to guide them.

Some of the characters and their names will seem very familiar to those you identified from the Child list of personalities. Notice

how the characteristics have become a more absolute, justified declaration of persona in Adolescence. The defenses are stronger, more
emphatic and live in statements such as, "That's just the way I am."
You may choose personal names for the personas that emerge from
your research. Remember that the character naming is never to be
used to shame or humiliate yourself or another.

Mildred the Martyr dominates with caretaking efficiency and
control but is burdened by the lack of recognition for all that she
does. Mildred is ultimately responsible for everything except her
own emotional overwhelm. Someone else is surely to blame for that.
Mildred's voice is heavy with weighted sighs and moans. "Why is it
always my job? Why can't anyone else do it and do it right for once?
When do I get to relax and rely on someone else?"

Herb the Heavy dominates with righteousness and indigna-
tion. He rules with a heavy fist and never-ending rules of perfection. His fear of looking foolish or making a mistake drives him to
be rigid and unbending.

Betsy the Bag Lady is poverty-stricken saving everything and
anything for a rainy day. Like many who survived the Depression
Years, the bag lady keeps everything, feeling that one day it may
have a use. She perceives others' throw-aways as treasures. Getting
rid of perfectly good clothes, dishes, linens and whatever else she
has collected is impossible, even if she has no use for it herself. Betsy
could die with a significant amount of money in her bank account
but would never have thought it was enough.

Oscar the Outrageous is known for having a passion and energy that overwhelms and exhausts others. He is always in action
and pushing for others to join him in over-the-top antics and projects.

He may initially enroll others with his high-spirited energy, but soon others withdraw when they realize that he is always initiating ideas without producing results.

Sally the Sassy Socialite can dance her way into and through any situation without ever being really known by anyone, including herself. Sally would never reveal any opinions or comments that would engender anyone else's displeasure.

Ralph the Righteous has an opinion on almost anything. Ralph can point to the reason for his upset and project the cause onto someone else. His body gets puffed up and stiff in his most pompous posturing. In Ralph's presence, others feel as though Ralph carries a large rule book that they will never be able to understand or predict. Ralph speaks as though he has a direct line to the Divine. "Everybody knows that this is unacceptable. You should have known what the policy is."

Pasha the Passionate is intense about everything she is involved with. She is dramatically engaged and vocal about every activity and relationship in which she interacts. She is quite artistic, often in many domains. She wears unique makeup and clothing that have her stand out in a crowd. She knows that she is special and wants everyone to recognize her accordingly.

Alvin the Avoidant is unable to take risks and step out of the box of fear in which he lives. He may be very intelligent, always thinking and considering, but seldom taking action. He is introverted and known for being a quiet observer.

Velma the Victim finds any reason possible to justify why her life is in a pathetic condition. "I tried," and "You just don't understand," are frequent mantras. If there is something that can go wrong, it will go wrong in the presence of Velma. Someone else is always to blame for her poor fortune.

Reggie the Rebellious will counteract any rule or authority with which he interacts. He hears a direction or a "should" and reacts with a debate justifying the reason for not doing things that way. Reggie has little energy available to create because he is always reacting and resisting being dominated and controlled.

Alice the Active is afraid of being left out and having no one to play with. She fills her life with projects and activities. She is a "do-do machine," always having something to do, somewhere to go, someone to visit. She will surround herself with many people and relate to all of them with a similar level of intimacy. Having many options of things to do and people to be with, Alice can always protect herself from the perceived pain of being alone.

Summary

Identify the characters that may look familiar to you from the above list and continue to reveal the characteristics of other personas and give them your own personal naming. Once you can recognize the personality and its impact, you are left with an opportunity to decrease its power in your life, if you focus the energy in a different direction. Notice the motivation of the persona: why it was developed and what it is trying to protect. When the issue can be healed, reinterpreted and redesigned, the personality may lessen in intensity, and the Adult can choose a more effective behavior.

Adolescent

Role: To be the Actor under the direction of the Adult; is heavily influenced by peers; important to release roles of script-writer, director, audience and critic.

Voice Indicator: Nasal, defensive.

Eyes: Shifting, confrontive, avoidant.

Caution: Beware of the Martyr role; drama, burden, blame and suffering; rules, justifications, expectations, absolutes and righteousness; Mr./Ms. Fix-it.

Feeling Mantra: "I am not enough."

Sylvia Sultenfuss

The Adolescent Wounding

At some point in adolescence there comes a time of wounding, a demarcation from childhood. Perhaps it was a seemingly perfect childhood, without stress, without expectations of responsibility. Perhaps it was an imperfect and stressful childhood, one in which there were hopes that someday things would change and work out. The wounding, this incident or series of incidents, communicates loud and clear: the Adolescent is truly on its own; there is no one else to rely on, and it cannot turn back or lean on the grownups around it to design the future it envisions. The wounding is incredibly painful and often frightening. It alters reality as it has been and shifts the sense of certainty forever. The wounding pierces the cloak of perfection and breaks the illusion of being indestructible, of being safe. The Adolescent fire for life is diminished; the passion is doused. The trust that safety will be provided by someone else is dashed. The wounding creates a break in the childlike trust of the Divine who was to provide the necessary protection, love and support.

For some, the wounding is a significant, memorable crisis that is obvious and historical — such as a death, a loss of a relationship, a move away from friends and family, a particular humiliation that damaged self-esteem. For others, the incident may have been something seemingly insignificant, unnoticed by others, or it may have been just another in a series of painful events that happened to be the one that ultimately broke the fiery spirit. The delicate balance of survival was broken, and the Adolescent was left raw and vulnerable to pain. It was no longer invincible. The seemingly impenetrable walls of defense could be penetrated. The Adolescent shifted from a position of exploration and expansion to one of protection and defensive posturing, determined never to be in a position to be vulnerable to this much pain again. The Adolescent developed an Actor persona, a personality that can retreat into a cave of safety or one who dances the dance in public but seldom exposes itself to being hurt again.

The wounding occurs for everyone traveling this human journey.

Though brief in time, its impact is significant and lasting. For me, my brother's death when I was thirteen (he was twelve) years old left a permanent mark on my sense of being safe from harm and death. He and I were buddies. Because we were closest in age, we spent many hours together exploring the woods and fields. We played endless imaginary games and sometimes were punished for our antics. We were playing with the cat just minutes before the accident that left him burned over 90% of his body. I heard his screams. I saw the burned flesh, and I felt his panic and shame.

Perhaps my father's frustration was spoken from the helplessness he felt in the moment. The message I heard and felt was his rejection of my brother as his anger about the accident exploded. "That damn kid!" I heard him say, "How many times have I told him not to play with fire?" In that moment, I decided that I would not lean on my parents to grieve, to share my feelings or ask questions that might challenge their feelings.

For two weeks, Jim lay in the hospital with Mom by his side. Both were visibly missing from our home. Dad continued to go to work each day, and we all had our summer chores. My eldest sister became the substitute home manager, and there was a hushed silence throughout the house. When the phone rang, I would listen intently for any clues of Jim's condition. Was he asking to see me? Would he come home soon? Would I get to see him? I asked a million questions to find out about Jim's burns and the treatment.

One day I was allowed to visit Jim in the hospital. Even though I was not yet fourteen, the legal age for hospital visitors, I relieved my mother so she could go home for a while. Jim slept peacefully. His body was wrapped in white gauze from his neck to his toes. His face was untouched. His hands were almost healed from the minor burns. The stench of rotting flesh was nauseating. For a brief moment Jim opened his eyes and told me to feel free to eat anything that was there in the room. It was as though he had felt my hunger and peeked out of his unconscious stupor to respond. No matter how I wanted to taste something, the oppressive odor intruded making it impossible. That was my last memory of my brother alive.

When the call came to the house to get my father to the hospital immediately, my sister understood the warning and moved all of us into action to get in the car. When we met my father at my grandmother's house, he collapsed sobbing into my grandmother's arms. I had never seen my father cry. The moment was over quickly as he removed his work clothes for his Sunday going to church clothes.

Entering the hospital, the troupe of us, my brothers, sisters and my father, waited for the elevator to take us to the second floor. The door opened, and there stood my mother and the nun who was the hospital administrator. "It is over," she whispered matter of factly. "He's gone." The silent shock suddenly vacuumed away the frightful anticipation of being able to say goodbye. We were escorted to the hospital room where I had visited Jim just a couple of days before. "Go and see your brother," the nun with a heavy Dutch accent coerced. "He is an angel now." I refused, no matter how much she pushed my fragile body. I'm sure I would have cursed my anger if I had known how to. No one could force me into that room to see my brother lying dead on the pristine white hospital sheets.

When Dad broke down crying at the wake, my mother shushed him whispering, "Not here. Wait until we get home." Even at the grave site, no one cried. I yearned to explode and wail for the loss of my brother. Why were tears not allowed? How did everyone else know the rule about not crying? Why would we celebrate the loss of my brother with a picnic shared by all the relatives? I ran to the woods, to the covering of the trees and brush and sobbed. "This is crazy," I screamed where no one could hear me.

Left alone to grieve without others' validation, I survived by stuffing away my feelings, too complex and painful to decipher. I decided that I would never need to lean on anyone again. My personality, its strengths and weaknesses, were permanently set in a wall of protection that became invisible and forgotten to me. Not having or communicating any depth of emotion just became a declaration of "that's just the way I am." It wasn't until I was studying the process of grieving in graduate school that I realized how many emotions had been blocked and never released. As part of the healing process, I made new declarations about being free to emote and communicate my own feelings.

I took my new discoveries and promises to my mother, asking the many unanswered questions. Why the grieving had been so silent and private; she could not answer. "We never had a death in our family before. I only remember that your dad never was able to cry after I stopped him that day in the funeral home. And when I began to cry six months after Jim's death, my sisters asked me when I was going to be done with the grieving."

Mother had felt lost and unprepared for this loss and grieving process too. My parents' ignorance and family patterns had never prepared them for the painful emotions they experienced. The Adolescent me could now forgive them and begin to heal. I could begin to understand my father's response to his own helplessness and pain. I could comprehend the inability to grieve in public, given my parents' upbringing.

As a result of these conversations, Mom and I designed a new agreement for addressing any future loss, a promise that would support both of us in grieving fully whenever that next time came. Our promise to each other served us well when my father died suddenly two years later. Arriving home, I found my mother had been given tranquilizers. She looked at me and begged, "I told you I wanted to feel everything this time."

I understood her meaning, took the medication away and made sure she drank plenty of fluids to release the powerful medications that were inhibiting her from feeling emotionally and physically. When her younger sisters came to visit, they were uncomfortable again with her sadness and tears and intruded with their protective guidance. "Marge, we need you to be strong just like you were when Jim died."

The sacred grieving contract called me forth to intervene. "If you are uncomfortable with her crying, please leave the room. She needs to grieve." They were not pleased with my intervention, but they did leave. My mother made requests that would allow her to grieve the loss of her husband of 45 years, and I supported those requests. Each family member was supported in expressing feelings. The tears, the anger, the questioning, the fears, the pain and terror were all allowed to be expressed as valid and important in our healing. The pain of my father's death was acknowledged without placing a defensive wall around the emotions, without replaying the defensive patterns of the Adolescent. My adolescent wounding was not repeated. The healing that had occurred two years before had allowed me a new way of grieving.

When reviewing our teenage years, some people recognize a pattern of being teased, a series of physical beatings or sexual intrusions, yet have no sense of which particular incident would have been the wounding event. We often know the day, the time and the exact incident when the behavior stopped, when a personal stand was taken. In that moment, the teen says, "No more!" and decides that it will lean on no one else, that to rely on oneself is the only way to survive.

Men often tell me about the day during their teen years when they stopped wrestling with their fathers. In some moment, both father and son realize that the teenager was now big enough and strong enough to dominate the grownup. The physical fights ended on that day. For women, the wounding is often related to or occurs near the time of their first menstruation when the responsibility for potential pregnancy and motherhood is realized.

The wounding usually occurs sometime during the teen years, after the onset of puberty. For some children, who are more dependent on their parents through high school, college and graduate school, the wounding is sometimes delayed into their twenties. A twenty-four-year-old client reviewed her life to discover her wounding. She described an idyllic childhood, growing up in a small town in which everyone knew her. The youngest of five children and the only girl, she was beautiful, talented, athletic and outgoing. Her family was active in the church and community, and all of her wants and needs were provided for. Her brothers protected her from any harm throughout her school years. She had a storybook relationship with her high school boyfriend, culminating in a beautiful wedding celebrating their perfect life together. They moved across the country to a big city and both got good-paying jobs.

Then one day, out of the blue, her high school sweetheart husband matter-of-factly informed her that he was leaving her. When she asked why, he answered that he was bored; that there was nothing real or authentic in their lives; that he didn't even really know who she was. There was no other woman or situation calling him away from the marriage, just his desire to find something real. She was left devastated and suicidal. The greenhouse protection that her family and community had so carefully provided had left her unprepared to deal with the challenges of life.

Within weeks of her husband's departure, the young woman discovered that her family was in a severe financial crisis. Her father had developed his own business, in which all his sons had joined as they got older. She learned that her father was in severe debt and unable to pay his bills. He had been maintaining an illusion of wealth, and now the house of cards was collapsing. Her whole world, everything she had held as real and true, collapsed; there could be no return to the illusion of safety. Her adolescent wounding had been delayed until she was 24 years old.

Summary

After the wounding of the Adolescent, there is an emotional loss, a break in the security of what we thought was real, secure and well-defined. This break results in a sacred wounding and in a declaration that we are alone, that survival is in our hands. We feel as though the spiritual trust we might have had in our parents and teachers, in our relationship with religion and the God of the child and adolescent no longer works in keeping us from pain and despair. Before the break in spiritual trust, there had still been a hope that everything would one day make sense and work out. Whatever had been painful, confusing or frightening would somehow be explained and be healed. After the break in trust, self-preservation and security become the most prominent underlying motivators.

The wounding is a time that seems to seal the fate of our patterns and beliefs designed to help us survive. Within the wounding is the data that can reveal a significant number of survival decisions that have held the individual's persona intact throughout the years. It is a hologram of the survival patterns. In healing and reinterpreting the beliefs and decisions made during that painful time, significant amounts of energy are released for use in designing a conscious new reality. The natural passion and talents of the Adolescent may begin to be expressed in a healthy and powerful way under the direction of a consciously designed Adult.

The Researcher/Observer

Following Adolescence comes a time when it is natural to be drawn to move out of the nest of home, out of the perceived security of family, school and community. It is a time when there is a surge of energy that calls us to generate a separate and unique life and to design who we want ourselves to be. If the journey has been a healthy one, if the person has processed through enough of the Child and Adolescent defenses, the choice to move forward is motivated by a natural calling of the spirit to leave home and claim the right to design a self-fulfilling life...a career, a job, a relationship.

Sometimes the decision to leave is made from desperation, with false hopes of a life without struggle or pain, in an attempt to escape a situation filled with anguish, resentment and hurt. Many have done whatever they must do to get away from angry parents, from deprivation and abuse, only to find themselves entrapped in the same kind of mess from which they have removed themselves. The false love and attention from someone else may give enough reason to leave an unloving environment. A demanding and overbearing parent may motivate one to prove that success is within reach, only to discover that the internal demands of self-perfection feed the internal messages of "never enough." The hope for success becomes more elusive than ever.

Some young adults are unprepared for the necessary separation from parents and home. Having seldom taken care of their own needs, they are blind to the tasks required for daily self-sufficiency. Many may never have had a job, earned their own money, washed their own clothes or made meals for themselves. Ill-equipped with the tools necessary for sustaining independence, they return to their parents or parent substitute for money, for a home and for their identity. The conflict of being age-appropriate for separating from parents yet returning to live in circumstances similar to that of the Adolescent creates confusion, anxiety and upsets. The reluctance to leave the perceived security and comfort of home or college can be immobilizing. Encouraging the fearful, young adult to be on their own, to get a job, a place to live and to make and manage their own money is essential. The process of individuation from parents is necessary and healthy in separating from the family of origin.

Often, the departure from family has not been well-designed. Parents may be unsupportive. Individuals may behave impulsively, under the influence of their friends or wanting to live out their fantasies of independence. Going off to college may be a scripted expectation following graduation from high school. College may be part of a plan to continue on with high school friends. College may fulfill a desire to attend a parent's alma mater. Going off to college can move one toward a healthy and successful individuation but it also may be tainted with Adolescent energy and parental pressure. College brings with it the enticement and pressures of parties, alcohol and other chemicals, and sorority and fraternity requirements, in addition to the demands of education and grades. The young adult is defining and redefining itself, different from the Child that accepted and lived in the parents' shadow, different from the Adolescent who rebelled from parents' expectations. Making decisions that are safe and effective in defining self and that are unique from parents and peer group is a constant challenge. Trial and error experiments accompanied by painful woundings are found along the path as the young adult designs an effective Researcher/Observer.

When my son decided to leave home and go off to college, he was adamant that he go far enough away to invent a new person, one that had no resemblance to the Adolescent high school student. He knew that he would be able to design himself more freely if separated from the influence of his high school friends and his mother. He decided to change his last name and invent a whole new image in an environment where no one would know him or have preconceived ideas about who he was or was supposed to be. His determination was clear, and the yearnings were healthy and natural. My son experimented with music, new friends and interests, dating, and managing his own time, money and responsibilities without any direction from his mother.

For many, the constructing of the Researcher/Observer originates after college when the young adult gets its first professional job, decides to get married and has a home of its own. Often the forced financial dependence on parents through college and graduate school extends through Adolescence into the late twenties and early thirties. For some, the period of exploration is cut short with demands that require a level of responsibility that does not allow for open-ended research. An Adolescent single parent raising a child or a couple that get married in or right out of high school do not have the same resources or opportunities for researching open-ended possibilities. These young people often slip quickly into an Adult by Default reality, feeling burdened with responsibility and with limited freedom to do otherwise.

The mission of the young adult is to design blueprints for new dimensions of possibilities, to safely explore new identities and ways of being, and to stretch the boundaries that have been defined by past experiences and decisions. If the young adult is given the opportunity to freely and safely explore, a competent Researcher/Observer will be developed. The Researcher/Observer must be free to not know in order to explore without restriction. If the Researcher/Observer does not have permission to not know, to live in the midst of inquiry, it will feel bored, immobilized, stifled and entrapped. It will quickly return to the reactive behaviors of the Adolescent who resists not knowing, and who will impulsively rebel and make it up rather than feel imprisoned. The voice is speculative and interested. The eyes look inwardly introspective and externally observant.

The mantra of the Researcher/Observer is "Life is interesting."

Providing the young adult with opportunities to explore beyond the requirements and restrictions of home is important in following a healthy path of designing a competent Adult. The freedom to research and explore is critical in completing past identities, in releasing past defensive posturing and descriptions of "that's just the way that I am," and in designing new possibilities of expressing and defining oneself. Out of a healthy process of discovery, individuation and redesign evolves a Researcher/Observer who is available for continuously exploring life and its meaning.

When I was nineteen years old and in the last semester of my sophomore year of college, I began to explore whether I had really chosen my career in nursing and whether I liked or appreciated the Catholic female college I was attending. Had I really researched my career and college or had I decided them by default? When in high school, I leaned toward psychology. The vice-principal guided me away from being a psychologist because it was primarily a profession of males. According to her, it would have taken too many years and too much money to get a PhD. In the end, I chose nursing and even then, she counseled against a baccalaureate degree: "Just go to a one-year or three-year program so you can get out soon and be making money." She was guiding me toward the predictable future of most young women my age: get married, have a family and work in the local hospital.

Having worked as a nursing assistant at the small hospital in my home town, I enjoyed the complexity of health care, appreciated interacting with a variety of people and recognized that nursing could give me the flexibility to work anywhere in the world. Everyone could use a nurse. So pragmatically, nursing would fulfill my basic requirements for flexibility, freedom to travel and financial independence. So, I wondered, had I truly chosen to be a professional nurse, or was it a decision made by default considering the limited options that were familiar to me?

Choosing a Catholic women's college because I knew that my parents would approve, I decided on the college that was furthest from my home but still within the state. Living 200 miles away, my parents would seldom come to visit and I would not be expected to come home on weekends. Not knowing anyone else who was going to the same college was exciting for me. I was ready for new friends and new opportunities. The tension began to rise in my second year of college. While I had good friends, was making good grades and had a full financial and work scholarship, I felt that I was living in a sheltered world that did not allow me to test my own values and character. Doors were locked by 10 p.m. on weekdays, midnight on weekends, and the lights were out by 11 p.m. — this was more restrictive than living at home with my parents. There were many students who tested the externally imposed limits, but for me, being unsafe or rebellious for its own sake was of little interest. Even in the secular colleges within the same city, dormitories were separated by gender with rules about doors being locked after certain hours.

I announced my decision to withdraw from school in the spring of my sophomore year. Faculty warned that I would not be accepted back into the nursing program, adding that I would lose my scholarship. My mother thought I was losing my mind and soul and required a visit to the local hospital administrator who was a Catholic nun. The administrator offered to provide the funding for me to complete my education, get my nursing masters degree and promised that she would open a mental health unit for me to manage upon graduation. I was firm. My decision was not related to anything the grownups around me identified as important. Discovering what was mine and what was not, as well as what values and principles I could count on without imposed rules and expectations of others was an urgent agenda for me.

I lived with a couple of girlfriends in an efficiency apartment. I worked at a big city hospital full time and took classes in music and psychology at the state university. I had plenty of opportunity to deal with exposure to alcohol, drugs, smoking and sex. Without the approval or guidance of the grownups in my life, I was required to finance myself and manage the impact of my decisions. What could I count on from myself? What was real and what was illusion? What mattered? At the end of the year, I returned to the same college with my full scholarship intact to complete my nursing degree. After a year on my own, I acknowledged that I had chosen a career that mattered to me. Altering the motivation for my choices and actions profoundly changed the way I related to everything. I now had a focus, a direction and clarity of purpose.

If the young adult is given the opportunity to research and explore without restriction or judgment, the process continues until there is a natural resolution to the confusion. As a result, Adult principles and character are produced, laying a foundation for an ever-expanding future. When the young adult has evolved to a healthy Researcher/Observer, the Conscious Adult has a full partner and is continuing the research of life and all of its possibilities. Revealing and designing matters of importance that are congruent with life principles can become a way of life. The Conscious Adult can ask challenging questions, and the Researcher/Observer can focus attention on discovering new distinctions and options for designing life.

The muscle of the Researcher/Observer may be called on throughout life as challenges, and limiting beliefs interfere with a healthy flow of living. When I opened a business with two partners who left in the first six months, I was left with significant financial responsibilities and little income to cover them. My relationship with money would have to expand. If I focused directly on questions of how to get more money or why this happened, I was left feeling immobilized and in panic. As I explored the meaning of money and the resources I had to bring in money, limiting beliefs about money became visible: "No pain, no gain." "Money means power." "Wealthy people have questionable integrity." And "Men manage businesses, women manage homes."

To expand my beliefs so that new possibilities would be available, I presented myself with challenging declarations that demanded a different perspective about money and business. Each month, a new statement of exploration was designed. The declarations and questions allowed me to focus on elements that mattered and would allow money to grow without focusing directly on how to get more money. One declaration was "Money is integrity. What will strengthen my integrity?" When a concern about money revealed itself, I would look into my life to identify areas of weak integrity. I would balance my checkbook, review the bookkeeping of the business and client billing and have healing conversations with those from whom I was withholding my upsets or judgments.

Another month the declaration was, "Money is love. In what areas am I withholding or blocking the giving and receiving of love?" Again, I would reveal the opportunities for expressing more love and in acknowledging the caring love that was supporting me, even if it didn't match my expectations. The research soon revealed the many blessings that were being denied and rejected or that were invisible to me. Allowing others to help, acknowledging others for their concern and support and asking for assistance from others opened unfamiliar territory for me. The willingness to research and the competence in asking powerful questions continued to open new distinctions and possibilities.

Summary

When the Researcher/Observer is integrated fully under the guidance and direction of the Conscious Adult, it can effectively explore a variety of interests and open many doors to unknown possibilities. The Conscious Adult can ask that the Researcher/Observer investigate what it means to function as a Conscious Adult, what it means to live with integrity and authenticity. The Adult can refocus the energy of fear to that of exploration and freedom from limiting and restrictive beliefs.

During the young adult period, life continues to reveal its lessons and trials. Issues of belonging and being loved, of being successful and feeling confident continue to reveal themselves. Breakdowns and losses continue to occur throughout life's journey. Oftentimes, the upset and pain of the losses, failures and humiliations trigger a defensive retreat to the protective warrior defenses of the Adolescent. The Adolescent has already proven itself successful in surviving the tough and unpredictable emotional journey of living. Adolescent tools of survival may be reinforced and strengthened with the pain of the young adult and the unfettered freedom to explore may be lost, or at least stifled. When the process of young adulthood does not produce a competent Researcher/Observer, the result is an Adult-by-Default.

Researcher/Observer

Role: Under the direction of the Conscious Adult, explores and designs options and possibilities; appreciates not knowing.

Voice Indicator: Speculative, interested.

Eyes: Introspective, observant.

Caution: Beware of feeling stuck, confused, immobilized and bored; will default to the Adolescent or Grownup Adult by Default if not given the freedom to not know.

Feeling Mantra: "Life is interesting."

The Adult by Default

The Adult by Default becomes the one who can survive over the long haul. It is the one who has grown up and figured out how to be accepted by the world without having to defend choices and behaviors. Often in our youth we hear the question, "When will you grow up?" The grownup submits to the pressure, to the pummeling of the world and becomes an identity, a profession, a career, a job, a role or a name. Something happens in the evolution of the human being that has us decide to be a grownup Adult by Default, to be appropriate and to live within the expectations and boundaries set by others. The grownup Adult by Default has been designed by Adolescent-defined beliefs and patterns, and so it is survival driven, rule-based and uncomfortable with change. Perhaps the default design occurs when we turn 21 years old or when we graduate from high school or college. Perhaps it comes when we get married or have children of our own. Sometimes a loss of a parent or a crisis that demands a responsible choice calls forth the Adult by Default. For some, it may be an administrative, management or leadership position that requires one to fulfill the expectations of others. Whatever the precipitant, the result is a serious decision: "I had better grow up now."

When that decision is made, the energy and resources that are necessary to bridge the journey between the Adolescent and the Adult by Choice are cut short. The result is that we settle for something less risky, less demanding and less conscious. The opportunity for the Researcher/Observer to explore expansive possibilities has been suppressed. Ideally, the Adult Researcher/Observer experiments with a variety of new roles, new talents and presentations until something seems to fit. When the process is hampered before the effective and extensive research is complete, the Adolescent takes over, and the result is an Adult by Default. This grownup has lost passion, purpose and mission in life and lives from the predictability of duty, obligation and burden of responsibility. The Adult by Default relies on history to explain and justify why things are the way they are. It is important to remember that the Adult by Default is a grownup Adolescent who is lacking the tools of research and exploration.

The mantra of the Adult by Default is "I am doing the best that I can."

There is little encouragement in the world for the expression of authentic passion and excitement. If we spontaneously show our emotions or dare to share them with others, we feel the humiliation and embarrassment for having revealed ourselves so vulnerably. We are left to survive in a world of no agreement, without acceptance. The exposure and the resulting retreat are painful as old wounds are reopened. Often we accept the outside world's invalidation and reject or deny our own experience.

We may attempt to recreate and hold onto memories of certain times when we felt passionate, alive and juicy but find it impossible. Creating repetition and beliefs to hold the experience intact are unsuccessful. Instead, what remains is a memory, a snapshot or a report about what happened. Soon an Adult by Default emerges, one that reports about the happening. The Adult by Default begins to teach and preach to have others believe what it has determined is important. Gone is the fresh authentic experience of the original event. What was an opening into something beyond the expected, beyond the explainable and understandable becomes another precept that is wrapped in explanations and expectations. The voice of the Adult by Default is righteous, justifying and rule-based. The eyes appear firm yet flat and with little evidence of emotion.

There is no Adult by Choice without a language and freedom to be different, without a willingness to not know and a competence in research and exploration. A willingness to continue to be a beginner and to persevere in redefining values and beliefs is required to sustain the sense of a refreshing breakthrough. When Pablo Casals, a renowned cellist of the twentieth century, was being interviewed at age 80, he was asked why he still practiced six hours a day. He responded with, "I think that after all these years, I am just beginning to know the cello." Even after a lifetime of playing the cello, of having discovered numerous distinctions about the cello, of having great success and awards for his brilliant performances, Casals recognized the importance of living as a beginner...a masterful beginner. What possibilities exist for us if we engage in the study of this human journey with that same degree of commitment and passion?

Adults by Default are often involved in lives in which there is plenty of activity, with schedules and interactions with family and community. Life is often routine and even hum-drum unless there is a crisis that calls forth a novel response or a change in routine. Asking the question, "What's missing?" can generate a passion and consciousness of choice that gives life substance and juice. Without choice, we feel entrapped and hopeless, which over time may result in depression.

It has been easy for me to remember that conscious choice provides the juice in life after an experience I had while working for a summer in a Hawaiian pineapple cannery at age 22. Since I was responsible for putting the right juice in the right can, it was important for me to understand the direction from the man who brought the pineapple to my canning machine for processing. There were three options, Regular, Choice or Fancy. The man's accent was difficult for me to understand in the midst of the cannery noise. "Juice," he hollered. I already knew that I needed to put in the juice. "What kind of juice?" I asked. "Juice," he hollered while gesturing frantically. After this exchange went on for a couple of minutes, the exasperated man called over the area supervisor. They communicated easily, and the supervisor then interpreted to me, "Choice, Wahini, Choice! What's a matta you?" So to me, juice has forever meant choice.

Summary

What is missing in the Adult by Default is the commitment to continue to expand the exploration for fresh, abundant and cogent distinctions. Without the committed research, entropy occurs as the demand for stability and the status quo expands. We are always either contracting or expanding. We human beings will either consciously cause our expansion through investing in opportunities for discovery and research, or we will be forced into expansion because of crisis and change around us. There are no other realities available. Having a crisis may be our way of calling forth some new growth rather than dying in stagnation.

What possibilities exist for us if we engage as beginners and excited explorers in the study of this human journey? If we consciously cause our growth opportunities by challenging ourselves with new learning experiences, with seminars, books and courses that are beyond our current comfort level, perhaps there will be less need for crises that demand our growth. If we stimulate our own change and are committed to our own growth, the Adult by Default has little power in our lives.

Adult by Default

Role: Grownup designed by the adolescent who lives out of old beliefs and patterns. Is survival driven, rule-based. Uncomfortable with change. **Voice Indicator:** Righteous, justifying, rule-based. **Eyes:** Firm, flat, little emotion.	**Caution:** Has lost passion, purpose and mission in life. Lives from predictability of duty, obligation and burden of responsibility. **Feeling Mantra:** "I'm doing the best that I can."

Sylvia Sultenfuss

The Conscious Adult

The distinction of the Conscious Adult by Choice may be difficult and illusive to identify. The voice of the Conscious Adult is strong, calm, direct, firm and clear. The resonance flows from the chest to the throat and flows naturally out of the mouth. The body posture is relaxed and comfortable, yet assertive and confident. The eye contact is steady and direct. The behavior is consistent, observant, creative and playful. The thinking is forward-looking and commitment-based. The Conscious Adult chooses and designs life from purpose, principles and possibilities. From vision and commitment, the Adult feels the freedom to design new futures.

The Adult by Choice lives the mantra "Anything is possible."

We may question whether the Adult lives anywhere in our lives, wondering whether there are any Adults in our world. There may be certain areas of your life in which you recognize the Adult by Choice as more present than others. In some domains there were no role models or at least, not ones that you chose to emulate. You were required to create from nothing, to generate possibilities about which you had no previous experience or information. You may have had to "fake it until you made it," but as a result you may have designed that domain using raw intuition and principles that have brought forward an Adult reality. Having no picture about how it "should" be, you experimented and explored until you were able to see the results that were aligned to your vision and principles.

If you were fortunate enough to have an Adult by Choice role model available to you in any domain of your life, consider yourself lucky. That person revealed to you the qualities of character, work-ability, authenticity and freedom. You saw the hope for achieving such a presence for yourself. Even so, you still have to design for yourself your own unique interpretation and reality of the Conscious Adult. The grownup Adult by Default reality occurs predictably in the journey of living. The Adult by Choice must be designed and revealed every moment of every day. The Adult only exists if you say so.

Sometimes we are thrust into designing ourselves without any history or previous mastery. When I first started my business with two other professionals, I had no experience in structuring or running a business. I went to accounting and real estate classes offered in evening community college courses so that I could at least have a language in conversing about those things that were a necessary part of doing business. I made many decisions based on what I thought was a good dose of common sense and intuition.

When my partners departed the business within the first six months of opening the doors, I was left with a three-year lease on four thousand square feet of space, with utility bills and salaries to pay. I was thrown so far out of my comfort and knowledge zone that there was no foundation on which to rely. I remember looking to the heavens and saying, "If this is what you want me to be doing, you'll have to help me." I declared my commitment to provide a place of integrity and honor for holistic health services. Throwing that commitment out ahead of my current ability to see or act allowed many opportunities to reveal themselves.

I told people the truth about my limitations and revealed my vulnerabilities. Asking many questions and listening for clues to guide me, I looked to others for information beyond my spectrum of knowing. Looking back, it was my commitment and my willingness to communicate openly that opened doors for miracles and gifts beyond my logic and control. It's not that I didn't put in lots of hard work. It's that by itself, hard work would not have been enough to sustain the business. Within the next six months, other health care providers and businesses stepped forward to fill the space and support the payment of bills. They came to me without my having known about them. It was as though they were called forth to use the office space as an opportunity for them to design their businesses.

I know there were many times during those months and beyond that the Child me was afraid, panicked and overwhelmed. Often the Adolescent me stepped forward with a good act of confidence to support me. However, my commitment was made from a place of soul, of Adult by Choice. I knew that I could not sustain the business without others' support and without divine intervention. I trusted that if having a healing center was part of my spiritual journey, it would come to fruition as long as I listened and continued to behave consistently with my commitment. My job was to keep my promises and do the work that was in front of me to do. That was almost twenty-five years ago. The business has adapted and transformed itself many times over those years. Although the people involved and the structure of the business have changed along the way, the commitment has flourished and taught me more than I ever could have imagined.

No matter how many times I remind myself and others that the Adult by Choice does not and cannot exist unless we create it every day and every moment, the desire for a quick fix may be stronger than words and good intentions. Within weeks of a breakthrough in creating a Conscious Adult, clients return to me disappointed, realizing the importance of additional coaching. I remind them that if they were learning a new language, they would give themselves at least a year of learning and practice before they could be expected to have a basic level of competence. The conscious generating of the Adult requires a memory muscle that gets stronger over time, but still requires the choice to make it happen. Eventually, the resonance and experience of the Adult by Choice becomes more real and more comfortable than that of the Child, Adolescent or the Adult by Default. To live from any other resonance becomes painful or uncomfortable. Besides, there is so much clean-up that must occur after the Child and Adolescent are in charge for any period of time that it is simply easier to keep the Conscious Adult present.

Some people have a surprising reaction of boredom when the Adult by Choice is present more consistently. The past pattern of addiction to drama and crises has held a significant amount of time and attention in their lives. They have asked for a change, recognizing that the intensity of the drama and suffering also causes significant damage and energy drain. After months of weekly coaching that focused on redesigning herself into an Adult by Choice, one client came to me and said, "I think that my Adult is much more present. People are remarking on how changed I am. They find it so much easier to work with me. But there is one big problem — I'm bored. There is no excitement or drama in my life." The domination and victimization patterns that she'd known for so long were no longer in charge of her life. For her, drama meant melodrama, and without it, life seemed too calm, too lacking in meaning and energy. When the Conscious Adult is more present than not, there can be an initial sense of loss of that to which we have become addicted. For this young woman, there was a new opportunity to bring forward authentic, Adult passion and excitement for life. That was new territory to research and explore.

Learning to live without adding more stress and drama to life's already predictable upsets and disruptions is a challenge. Designing a life that flows consistently with conscious choices and designs brings forth more ease and freedom in living. Life will continue to provide its pains, fears, changes and losses. Our choice to remove the melodrama and suffering is one that the Adult is able to make. There is an expression that states, "Pain is inevitable; suffering is optional." The Conscious Adult knows the difference.

The Adult continues to feel and express emotion without damaging justifications, blame or victimizing. Discovering the keys to the Conscious Adult's passion and commitment without the drama and soap opera of life is a challenge worth its demand. The Adult feels deeply and intensely. The Adult embraces the emotional self and communicates without the bravado and melodrama of the Adolescent. When the Child and Adolescent are fully embraced by a competent Adult by Choice, all feelings and emotions are available to be experienced. The expression of these feelings lives in the Adult's choosing. The Adult can feel deeply without expressing the emotions dramatically. The way one expresses emotions can be chosen. Imagine being able to be satisfied and full of life no matter what the external circumstances. When you live life from the freedom of choice and commitment rather than knee-jerk reaction, a new quality of life is available at every moment. In the beginning, it may seem difficult to sustain consciousness. Just like starting any new training, the commitment one makes to the practice and change is critical. Committing to at least a year of retraining, to learn a new language and to alter behavior patterns is called for in designing a competent Conscious Adult. Being competent in the ability to use one's energies, gifts and talents for making a difference in the quality of living is worth the research. Having peace of mind, heart and soul is worth the commitment. Experiencing the freedom of choice and self-expression is worth having come to the game board of Humanity. We have already experienced the alternative: a life of reactivity and drama that is determined by the circumstances and the pre-defined beliefs of our past. We continue to yearn for a balance and fullness in our lives.

We may continue to resist birthing and sustaining the Conscious Adult because it can feel frightening and painful to lose the past identity. In any grieving and healing process, there are levels and phases of healing; this is also true in the revelation and birthing of the Adult. The defensive posturing that has protected us from discomfort and separation for all these years was put in place for a good reason. Each time there was a similar threat of pain, the current upset was stuffed away into the recesses of the mind — into the locked areas of the subconscious library.

When we begin to recognize that we do not have the level of

intimacy, joy, peace and abundance in our lives that we have yearned for, and when we begin to acknowledge the fears and beliefs that are blocking us from having what we want, the pain that has been walled up begins to emerge. The painful memories that have been stored in the cellular structure begin to emerge as real physical and emotional aches and discomforts.

Over many years, a client of mine had been confronting and releasing the grief of past losses and painful experiences in her life. Each release had given her more and more freedom and yet, left her yearning more and more for what was missing in her marriage. It was no longer viable for her to continue the patterns of bitterness and martyrdom, of default and blame, of shame and guilt. She experimented and tried to change herself and have conversations with her spouse about the destructive patterns in their relationship. The mutual blame and pain continued. She chose to separate physically from the relationship. It was then that she confronted the deep pain and horror of loss and abandonment that had entrapped her spirit her whole life. The pain was real. The pain was physical and emotional. The pain was spiritual as she realized her own part in the patterns of destructive communication. She could now begin to heal in a new way, with forgiveness and compassion for herself and her husband.

The grieving is not easy — just necessary if any other options for quality of life are to be designed. Freeing the energy that has been attached to the past history of losses and patterns of betrayal and abandonment allow us to design new futures and possibilities. Imagine that the soul has a contract with us to "get us home," to accomplish the goals we set out to achieve in this lifetime and to fulfill our destiny. We have a choice about how, when and if we accept the challenge. Settling for the illusion of comfort and calm, versus having authenticity and intimacy with self and others is always possible. The freedom to explore new ways of being is available when there is a conscious choice to do so — and choice always brings risk with it. There are no guaranteed results.

Often it feels as though we must let go of who we are in order to be a Conscious Adult. What we are required to let go of are the illusions of who we are — our personalities, our beliefs, our survival defenses, our cultures and our histories. These illusions are the prisons for the true self, for the vibrant, passionate self waiting to be realized. Many people describe the process of letting go and discovering a more real self as a personal emotional, physical and spiritual dying. We find it hard to imagine who we could be without our old defenses. We have defended ourselves for so long with "that is just the way I am," that we believe that our patterns are us, are who we are. It is only when there is a letting go, when there is a separation from the old patterns, that there is a space for new creations and opportunities. It is when the cup is emptied that there is room for more juice. The important thing is to consciously create what you want to put in the space that is made available when you release the energy attached to the past. Otherwise, the old familiar patterns will quickly fill the space again. Holding the vision of the possible new life, new opportunities, new ways of relating and living, will provide the foundation for releasing the no longer useful beliefs and structures on which we have depended for so long. Imagining what could be possible gives us hope to come out of the old paradigm and build a foundation for a new self to emerge. Oftentimes the process of releasing is painful and requires a healing forgiveness.

The Conscious Adult and Distinctions of Commitment

My husband of fourteen years one day informed me that he had chosen not to be married and wanted his freedom. Since I had perceived our relationship as more secure than ever before, I was stunned. It was time to figure out why I was married to a man who wasn't clear that he had chosen me, our marriage or our family. I was aware that I had heard these messages before and had always worked to change myself, to alter my way of relating and living life. This time my own patterns and decisions that placed me in this situation must be revealed and healed. Even when my husband declined counseling, I went to work on myself. I had no doubt that I had made a conscious lifetime commitment to this man and to our relationship. To have both threatened to be taken away without my permission was unacceptable.

Looking deeper, disgust emerged about who I had become within my marriage. In order to keep peace with my husband, I had let go of friendships and activities in my life that had mattered. I took care of everything from the meals to the laundry, from the yard work to the painting, from the bookkeeping to the maintenance of equipment. Holidays were prepared with decorations and celebrations. Even though I worked full time outside the home, working full time at home was also necessary. Becoming a martyred, lone ranger caretaker of household and family was the result. I was no longer the person that my husband had married. I was no longer the person that I envisioned living my life. While I had tried to live out my expectations about what would create a happy home and family, my husband had been excluded. All he could voice was what he didn't want. When it appeared that he was unable to tell me what he did want or expect, I decided for both of us. I had no idea that he didn't know how to do the things I wanted him to participate in. When I chose him to be my husband, I was aware of some of our differences in background and patterns of communicating feelings. I functioned under the belief that if I loved him enough, more than all others had in his life, his scars would heal so that he could express his love and responsibility fully. Unconsciously, my patterns fulfilled the psychological profile of a co-dependent woman who demanded that commitment was forever and that I alone could make anything work.

When I began to own my resentments and the punishing anger that was cloaked in my declaration of love, my belief structure shattered, leaving me suffering and challenging everything that I had ever held as real. Was my whole life a sham? Was there nothing that was real and authentic? Was I really so blind and stupid? Could I ever heal the physical and emotional pain that seemed to be ever-present in every cell of my being? Could I ever trust myself again to make healthy choices? This was not the first time I had asked these questions in my life or in my relationship, but it was the deepest I had allowed myself to touch. Promising to confront whatever was necessary, I hoped that I would never have to undergo this fear, sadness, pain and shame again.

Every night before going to sleep, I would explore the incidents of pain and betrayal that had occurred in our relationship. Releasing every shred of emotional attachment that kept me bound to this man was my work. If I was free of the unhealthy attachment, I could then choose freely and consciously. After at least 30 nights, the slate felt clean. There was no more to reveal, no more to feel. A void was all that remained, a nothingness that left me wondering who I was and how I would go forward. This point of emptiness can be frightening. The not knowing and the vulnerability of feeling there was no certain structure that would support me left me feeling shaky, but at the same time clean and open.

When there had been enough healing and forgiveness, there was an opening for me to acknowledge the special and wonderful things in our relationship. Not everything had been horrible and painful. There had been times of great passion, compassion, intimacy in communication and loving, joy and sense of family with our son, and times of authentic sharing and exploration. What had not worked that kept us stuck in our ineffective patterns was becoming more evident. The patterns that had been designed by the Child me who was afraid of rejection and loss and the Adolescent me who was afraid of breaking the concepts and beliefs of what a good marriage, a good wife and husband looked like were becoming more and more clear. What did work in our relationship was the power of my love and commitment that allowed me to do significant work of revealing and healing in my life.

The process of researching and releasing continued for a full year before I was willing to sign divorce papers and declare the relationship complete. Complete did not mean finished or broken. Complete meant that I was able to be whole and allow the relationship to change form while I would continue to live from the love and commitment of soul. We could together parent our son and sustain a communication that honored and respected each of our choices and paths.

Claiming the gifts of this relationship and all that it had taught me allowed me to begin the process of consciously designing a new me. The self-development work of formal education, informal retreats and training, books and therapy had brought me to this place. My Conscious Adult being was present enough to reveal the pain and patterns without destroying me. My mind would never have allowed me to go to the depths of the hidden secrets and pain if I had not been prepared enough, if the Child and Adolescent parts of me had not felt safe enough. In an interesting way, I was able to acknowledge my husband for the gift of completion and the treasured self growth beyond anything I could ever have imagined.

During this process of healing and completion, my interpretation about commitment, family, parenting and relationship had to be redesigned. The form of a marriage that we had committed to as husband and wife who made a lifelong promise to live together was no longer viable. Could we sustain our commitment to emotionally and spiritually grow together and be responsible for family? I could not envision breaking the forever promise I had made on my wedding day.

How could I express my commitment of heart and soul while being realistic about redesigning the form of our relationship? New distinctions were required that could allow me to live out of my commitment of soul, yet release the promises that had been formulated during the history of our relationship. The unhealthy roles in which we had engaged and the broken promises had to be acknowledged. I could see the complex quandary that I was in but I had no idea how to sort out the particles.

The Distinctions of Commitment diagram reflects the results of my research to discover how to live out of my commitments without being bound by the beliefs and expectations that had strangled the life force at the source of these commitments.

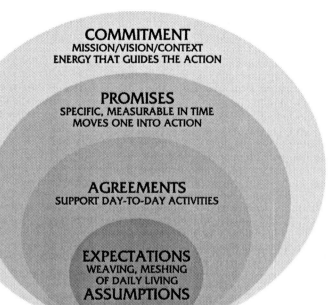

The outer circle of Commitment is the energy and force that guides the context of commitment. It is an energy that both pushes and pulls us toward something or someone. It continues to call us forth seemingly from our soul and spirit, without our understanding of why it does. In my marriage, I had been drawn to this man with an emotional force that I had never before experienced. Even though I had explored and analyzed our interaction for three years before getting married and had acknowledged the obvious difficulties that would challenge us, I had consciously chosen to marry my husband. For me it was a soul commitment that had demanded its opportunity to live. There were many times throughout our years of marriage that my husband and I discussed the depth of our calling to be with each other. We seemed to be aligned with so many principles and values, yet often we interpreted them quite differently. I sensed that we were together for a purpose beyond any that was rational. Our complex differences were many and yet, core elements of our values were powerfully aligned.

We often find the same kind of opposites in our friendships. We seem to be drawn to the variances as a way of balancing our own gifts and power. Perhaps there is a natural desire to learn from another about those areas that are less developed in our own repertoire. Others might challenge our friendships with persons that are so different but there seems to be an energy that draws people together that is seldom rational or explainable.

Within the context of commitment is the second circle of Promises. Promises are the content within the context; they are the form that is sourced from the energy of commitment. Promises are consciously and verbally made with oneself or another. The promises are the specifics of the marriage contract. They are measurable and tangible. They may be altered in the process of the relationship as required by circumstances, such as children, ailing parents, job loss, new career development and education. As the challenges appear along the journey, deciding how to respond requires interaction and alterations to the promises. A marriage vow such as, "I promise to love and honor you until death do us part" is a commitment without form, without specific and clear distinctions. The two people engage in the commitment without truly knowing what will be called forth in their journey together. Without communication, they are likely to assume their interpretations are the same.

In most marriages, there are discussions about who will be the breadwinner, if and when to begin having children, when to purchase a home, whether to move to a new home or city, all the decisions that life brings to us in the journey of relationship. In my own marriage, I realized that many critical issues were never brought to the table for discussion and thus, were never brought to the level of a promise. We either didn't know how to discern, or we didn't realize that something needed to be discussed. There seemed to be an automatic marriage journey script that we were following. It was just time to get a house. It was time to have a child. It was important to save money. We sometimes didn't realize the importance of exploring our different goals and points of view or to even recognize that there might be a difference. Consequently, there was plenty of room for expectations and assumptions to rule our conversations so that when there were breakdowns, the communication was blaming and painful.

Within any relationship promises have different valuations. Some are sacred and non-negotiable; they are deal-breakers. Others seem to maintain the stability of the relationship, a contract or a situation. If the promises have not been clarified with detailed discussions, there will be breakdowns about the interpretations and meanings. It is critical to discover what is being asked of you and to be specific about what you are asking of another.

Explorative questions and discussions will reveal many differences if we listen for them rather than listening for agreement. How one person defines any language may vary significantly from another and yet, each hears that they are in accordance because the same word is being spoken. What does it mean to be faithful? What does integrity mean? How do we value money? What does it mean to love and honor? Each of us has our own interpretations and some are held with a sacred energy of non-negotiability. Does the other person in the relationship share the same meaning? Do you have the same goals and expectations for achieving our goals? If the differences can be revealed and discussed, there is an opportunity for a negotiated resolution, one in which both parties feel valued.

Within the circle of Promises are Agreements. Agreements involve interactions that support day-to-day activities. It is often necessary to specify and alter the agreements in the design of the week or the day. Life's conditions often require changes. If the agreements are not brought to consciousness and renegotiated according to the needs of the situation, there will be breakdowns. Conversations about who will be responsible for mowing the lawn, picking up the children from school, getting the groceries and paying the bills are just a few of the items that require communication with anyone else who might be involved in the family activities. Who will be the one responsible for the social calendar, for planning vacations, for handling the finances, for keeping communication alive in the relationship? Oftentimes the roles and expectations are based on how our parents, teachers, friends and employers have fulfilled those roles in the past.

Within friendships the same discussions are necessary in identifying roles and competencies. Each relationship requires communication to clarify specific requests and expectations in each situation. Even when agreements have been made, alterations may be required depending on the availability of the persons involved and their competence and capability to fulfill the task. Again, many breakdowns can occur when the agreements become routine and habitual without an opening for discussion and renegotiation.

Within the circle of Agreements are Expectations and Assumptions. Expectations and assumptions become visible when there is a breakdown. Concerns have not been discussed with clear distinctions that both parties understand and agree to. No matter how specifically we think we have clarified our wants, needs, requests and promises, the measuring devices of the other person will never perceive, interpret, or create in the exact same way as we have. So often we hear ourselves say, "Everyone knows that behavior is inappropriate. Everybody knows that it is important to be on time. Everybody knows that it is important to save money. It's just common sense." Each of us has made these kinds of statements hundreds of times.

No one ever interprets reality exactly as someone else does, so assumptions and expectations cause significant and frequent breakdowns. Some people are talented at sensing the wants and needs of a situation or another person. Often we fall into the trap of assuming that whoever we are in relationship with can read our desires accurately and without having to make a request. If something is of value to you and you do not communicate it, there is a high probability that it will not be fulfilled. It is important to remember that everything lives or dies in our communication and that assumptions will predictably precipitate breakdowns and upsets.

Breakdowns and Upsets

The tension between a husband and wife was evident as they entered my office. The wife held her arms crossed over her chest, her jaws were tightly clinched, and she would not look at her husband. The husband displayed a jovial anxiety as he chatted about their week's activities. When I asked him if he noticed that his wife was upset, he quickly acknowledged it and responded, "She's been like that for three days and won't tell me what I did wrong."

The wife held resolute, refusing to tell why she was upset. "He knows why. He's just being coy."

Finally, I invited the wife to leave if she was not willing to participate. She then told her story. She had called her husband before he left work and invited him home for a romantic evening. The children were staying overnight at a friend's house, and she was preparing a special meal for them. He had responded with excitement telling her that he would be home in 20 minutes.

She described his coming in 45 minutes later, slamming the front door, stomping down the hallway, and not even responding to her solicitous "hello" from the kitchen. "He stayed in the bedroom for a very long time while I was putting out dinner. It was cold and ruined when he finally appeared all sweet and romantic."

The husband sat in disbelief as he listened to the wife's description. His story was quite different. He had left work immediately after his wife's call. He got stuck in traffic coming home and had rushed into the house because he had to use the bathroom. He had not heard his wife's greeting and decided to shower and get ready for the romantic evening. When he went to the kitchen to greet her with romantic gestures, his wife refused to speak or engage. Both husband and wife had their own experience and had invented reasonable stories about what had happened. Without sharing their interpretations, the upsets became more real, resulting in a severe break in communication. The opportunity for an intimate evening had been lost, but even more had been threatened.

Upsets often cause a reaction that is destructive to the foundation of a relationship. If we are unconscious to the impact of assumptions and expectations, we will blame the other person for having caused the upset. Often when there is a breakdown, we accuse the other of not being committed or of breaking a promise to us. We challenge the value and quality of the relationship and the commitment. We often react by discounting the person and the commitment without identifying the upset and the behavior that triggered the automatic reaction. We demand an apology and immediate change in behavior. "You have to promise to never do that again. You know how it upsets me." The truth is that no one can protect us from our upsets.

Generally, when we truly comprehend the meaning of the "trigger behavior" and the upset it causes for another, we do not consciously cause the betrayal, the loss or the breakdown. If the behavior or object of discussion was as important to another as to us, they would behave consistently with our priorities. Often the issues of upset are a personal, unconscious and undefined trigger that becomes evident only in the midst of the breakdown. It is our own personal button that is ours to heal or disengage, but instead we ask the other person to protect us from being upset, from being triggered. Upsets reveal triggers from past experiences, from our patterns of invisible expectations and assumptions. They spotlight our personal work for releasing emotional attachments and the importance we have placed on certain objects and behaviors. When we are conscious, we can accept our own role in the upset, reveal our own values and expectations and make requests of another to support us in a different way.

We can request that another person honor that these issues are important to us. We can ask them to promise, to the best of their ability, to refrain from pushing the trigger button. However, it remains our personal responsibility to do our own work to identify the issue, its meaning, what triggers the upset and why and to discharge the intensity of the triggered reaction. What might have been an understandable fear and defensive response of a Child is no longer healthy or necessary. The Adult by Choice acknowledges that there are unconscious cellular memories that can be engaged and that cause a reaction that is unrelated or inappropriate to the current situation. The Conscious Adult recognizes its responsibility to discover and unhook the triggers and minimize the reactive responses.

Summary

We will probably never be without reactive upsets. If there is no conflict or upset in a relationship, someone is dying, someone is dominating and someone is submitting. As long as we are relating to others, we will be triggered and our automatic reactive behavior will be revealed. Observing the upsets and working to release the beliefs that generate those reactions is life work for each of us. As we acknowledge that the issues are ours to work with and heal, we can begin to observe the triggers, our reactions and patterns of thinking that are connected to the discomfort. We can begin to identify and release the pain and fear that may have activated the patterns.

The key to understanding our beliefs and values lives in the research of our upsets. If something didn't matter to us, we wouldn't be distressed. Discovering how it matters and why it matters can reveal a source of old scars, damage caused by painful happenings in the past. The mattering might also reveal an important life principle that is core to the quality of our life. Being willing to explore any upset beyond the immediate reaction is an exploration and learning that brings more opportunity for healing and choosing. Designing and choosing to be a Conscious Adult at every moment is a challenge for the rest of our lives.

Conscious Adult by Choice

Role: Director, Manager, Coach.

Voice Indicator: From the heart to the throat, calm, direct.

Eyes: Direct eye-to-eye contact.

Caution: Must choose to design life from purpose, principles, possibilities, from vision and commitment. Important to feel the freedom to design new futures.

Feeling Mantra: "Anything is possible."

Distinctions of the Team Members

Child	
Roles: To have fun, be loved, secure and safe. **Voice Indicator:** High-pitched. **Eyes:** Open, expressive, averted when in shame.	**Caution:** Beware of raw emotions; panic/pain/rage; fight/flight behaviors and role as Victim. **Feeling Mantra:** "I never got enough."

Adolescent	
Role: To be the Actor under the direction of the Adult; is heavily influenced by peers; important to release roles of script-writer, director, audience and critic. **Voice Indicator:** Nasal, defensive. **Eyes:** Shifting, confrontive, avoidant.	**Caution:** Beware of the Martyr role; drama, burden, blame and suffering; rules, justifications, expectations, absolutes and righteousness; Mr./Ms. Fix-it. **Feeling Mantra:** "I am not enough."

Researcher/Observer	
Role: Under the direction of the Conscious Adult, explores and designs options and possibilities; appreciates not knowing. **Voice Indicator:** Speculative, interested. **Eyes:** Introspective, observant.	**Caution:** Beware of feeling stuck, confused, immobilized and bored; will default to the Adolescent or grownup Adult by Default if not given the freedom to not know. **Feeling Mantra:** "Life is interesting."

Adult by Default

Role: Grownup designed by the adolescent who lives out of old beliefs and patterns. Is survival driven, rule-based. Uncomfortable with change.

Voice Indicator: Righteous, justifying, rule-based.

Eyes: Firm, flat, little emotion.

Caution: Has lost passion, purpose and mission in life. Lives from predictability of duty, obligation and burden of responsibility.

Feeling Mantra: "I'm doing the best that I can."

Conscious Adult by Choice

Role: Director, Manager, Coach

Voice Indicator: From the heart to the throat, calm, direct.

Eyes: Direct eye-to-eye contact.

Caution: Must choose to design life from purpose, principles, possibilities, from vision and commitment. Important to feel the freedom to design new futures.

Feeling Mantra: "Anything is possible."

Sylvia Sultenfuss

Designing and Sustaining the Spiritually Conscious Adult

Each of us participates in creating the script of our lives and in doing so, calls forth the opportunity to discover the lessons and gifts along the way.

Just imagine that being human required us to have no memory of having participated in co-creating our lives once we came into the physical world. We would live life without fully realizing that we asked for certain lessons and challenges along the way. We wanted to learn, to discover and to expand our awareness of who we are. We challenged ourselves to reveal and design an Adult relationship with the spiritual. We demanded of ourselves that we learn about the power and distinctions of love. Our souls joined us in our commitment to learning our lessons and fulfilling our destiny.

Along the path of being human, there are many bumps and hurdles for each of us. Just imagine that we are spiritual beings with limitless, unbounded sources of energy who select to play the game of Humanity. The game requires boundaries, limitations and an ego whose purpose it is to make sure that we survive. There are predefined elements as in any game; rules, chance cards, rolls of the dice, decisions and scripts with characters and situations along the way. Just coming into such a game of life could be a painful and restricting experience for a limitless force of energy. Yet, the human journey is a most powerful and effective way for the soul to expand. As we travel the path of being human, we have opportunities to confront our limitations, pain and shame. We also have the opportunity to rewrite the scripts, to redesign the patterns and reinterpret the experiences and the decisions we made. We have the opportunity to choose to alter our perceptions and to claim the power of our spiritual heritage. Our souls may be allowed to sing with more freedom and power of voice.

Allowing the Child and Adolescent to be in charge in the grownup years will tend to generate upsets and crises. Life will continue to give us times of illnesses, accidents, losses and disruptions, so that our ability to reveal, embrace and deal with our vulnerability and pain will be exposed. We may respond to these situations with drama and panic if there is no Conscious Adult present. Such experiences may demand that we rethink and redesign our patterns of defense, or we may choose to avoid exploring the vulnerability and its gifts. If we make that choice, if we pull back and strengthen the walls of defense, then we limit our freedom of self-expression and choice. Growing older is mandatory in the human journey; becoming a spiritual Conscious Adult is always a choice.

Conscious choice is the key to living a Conscious Adult life. If we do not create the Adult at every moment of every day, the Adult will not occur.

We will not one day just wake up and have a wonderful, conscious, enlightened being running our lives. As we expand the recognition that we do, in fact, have a choice in designing and responding consciously to life's offerings, we begin to be more comfortable with the resonance of being conscious. Soon being unconscious and feeling as though we are at the effect of everything that occurs in our life begins to be less comfortable and less acceptable. No longer is it fun or satisfying. Being able to shift and reinterpret a situation and live with a sense of harmony becomes much more enticing. No matter how competent we become in designing a conscious life, we must continue to choose to be a Conscious Adult at every moment.

Once in a seminar I was conducting, a woman realized the inevitable, never-ending demand for us human beings to be conscious. She blurted out, "We are doomed." She was right. The demand to be conscious can be one of doom or one of interest and excitement about what might be possible. An upset client called one day and reported that her Adult was Missing in Action (MIA). We both laughed and understood the source of the chaos and melodrama that was playing itself out in her life given her descriptive report.

A man who was considering going into business with me asked, "You would require me to be conscious, right?"

"Absolutely," I said.

"Then the answer is no," he declared.

Will the conversation about being conscious be perceived as a problem or as a challenging opportunity?

How will we know that a Conscious Adult is present?
- We will sense our emotional and automatic reaction to a situation, and rather than allowing the reaction to rule, we

will behave consistent with our principles, with our best self and with our sacred values of how we want others to relate to us.

- There will be less drama and fewer messes to clean up, occupying our time and energy. Instead, our lives will be filled with our creative projects and activities that contribute to our quality of living.

- Others will value being in our presence. They will listen to what we have to say and begin to integrate our principles into their own thinking. They will describe feeling more valuable and having more impact. They will be looking for ways to make a difference. They will challenge us to expand.

- We will sense our passion for life and our vulnerability in living, and we will value both. Each can be expressed without drama and without placing blame or guilt. We recognize authentic freedom and power in making Conscious Adult choices.

As we expand our freedom of choice and build an authentic sense of power, we continue to research and explore the boundaries of our own limiting beliefs and perspectives. Continuing to ask questions that reveal the motivation and meaning behind a thought and/or behavior pattern opens new distinctions and options for choosing new behaviors.

Embracing feelings are key to discovering our spirituality and its meaning.

Instead of denying, defending or suppressing our feelings, we can now reveal and explore them to discover what the upset is about, to reveal why a reaction is so strong and to reclaim the power of the emotion so that it can be directed consciously. When we stop feeling, we are unable to reveal our vulnerability and our passions. When we block one emotion, we stifle all emotions, including the depth of our desires. Experiencing feelings allows us to reveal our humanity, our compassion and caring, as well as our concerns and values. Feelings lead us to our personal principles. Feelings unveil our hopes that life can be different and that we are not alone in this journey. Feelings allow us to discover more about our spiritual destiny. Without the ability to embrace our feelings, we begin to reject our humanity. We often feel shame about being human, wishing that we did not think petty thoughts, that we did not have opinions and upsets and that we were not so imperfect. When we acknowledge that we are spiritual beings playing a game, we can begin to have compassion for our humanity and that of others and begin to heal the shame we feel. The Human game board is the one we chose to play on to discover and reveal our spiritual heritage and our relationship with the Divine.

As you review your life, identify those situations and happenings that had significant impact on you. Allow yourself to dip into the feelings just enough to experience the pain, fear, shame and anger. It is important to take only one cupful of the emotions and process their meaning and begin to release the intensity of the mattering. If we dip too deeply or take too much of the emotion at one time, we may stir up more feeling and drama than we can handle or process successfully. Every situation and every cup of feelings is a hologram of the whole containing all the information we need to analyze our feelings, the decisions we made and our reactions to the dynamics involved in the situation.

At age sixteen, I was invited on my first boat ride. We traveled the Mississippi River of mid-Minnesota in the hot, July sun. I was feeling quite svelte in my new white bathing suit that reflected my toasty bronzing body. When we returned to the boat docks off the main waterway, my friend asked me to tie off the boat as she brought it in. Having never tied off a boat before, I reached up over the ledge of the bow and stretched to snag the loop of rope over the wooden stake on the pier.

Just as I was roping the stake, the boat captain revved the motor into reverse, and the boat jumped back as I leaned forward. Over the bow I went, falling into the murky water below. Never could I have imagined the slimy, stagnant gasoline and filth that was below. My legs promptly became embedded in a quicksand of sludge up to my waist. Every time I tried to kick free, I slipped even deeper into the mud. Remembering the old black and white TV movies that always admonished the cowboy to be very still when he got stuck in quicksand, I tried to relax. I could hear the hysterical laughter for what seemed to be at least ten minutes before my body finally decided to float to the top. The nasty taste and smell of the gasoline and filthy water remains in my memory today.

As I pulled myself onto the dock, thankful that I was alive and shamefully embarrassed at my faux pas, I was horrified at the slugs that stuck to my legs and the black slime that filled my swimming suit. I must have smelled as horrible as I appeared. I washed my new white bathing suit many times with soap and with bleach. Never did the original pristine white color return. Never did it smell clean and new. Finally, I threw the suit away.

The moral of this story: If we dig too deeply into the depth of the pain and shame, we can be left stuck and unable to resolve or heal the issues. If we experience too much pain, we may be unwilling to continue searching our past upsets, along with the patterns and decisions we made to protect us. In the past and current paradigm of psychology, the intent is to reveal and experience the feelings of the dark shadow and to bring some understanding and relief to the remembrance. The expectation is that the pain may always be there and that we will again slip into it. It is a matter of when, not if.

In the new paradigm of designing a Conscious Adult, we explore the feelings and meanings of the dark self and open the door to a light self, the self of possibility, of love and relationship with the Divine. We may be frightened to explore the new light self. We have become comfortable with our old psychological explanations and rationale for how and why we are the way we are. The point of greatest discomfort is the point of moving from the old paradigm to the new paradigm. We have not yet designed a trustable reality around the new self. Allowing ourselves to feel the joy, the freedom and the power of choice brings with it the fear of slipping uncontrollably back into the dark sludge of the past patterns.

If we master exploring the old self, one cup at a time, feeling the feelings, revealing the meanings that have been sealed in time and space, and healing, releasing and reinterpreting the past, we diminish its power. There is now an opportunity to focus the energy that has been released towards the design of new futures, new possibilities for self and for humanity. As we focus the energy on dreaming dreams, on designing new maps for ourselves, we expand the power and reality of the new paradigm for ourselves and for humanity.

Being complete and whole at all times, regardless of the circumstance or story, is significant in designing our sense of self and our perception of reality.

Often we have walked away from people and painful situations, unable or unwilling to resolve the emotional entanglement. The loss seemed too painful, the shame too deep and the damage too significant for us to deal with in the moment. We survive by stifling the deep, emotional energy and move on. Sometimes we may think that we will come back to heal the feelings at a later date, but we seldom do. The significant emotional void, the scar and the numbness remain.

When my brother died, I observed the grieving responses of those around me. No one cried, at least not publicly. In anesthetizing my own emotions, I was surprised in graduate school to discover that I had not processed the normal emotional stages of grief. Once I realized and healed the barriers to feeling my grief, I promised to allow the expression of emotions, mine and others', when death and loss occurred in the future.

When my father died suddenly a couple of years later, I felt the pain and the rage of loss. Having only three days leave from work after the funeral, I pulled myself together, put on my "I'm OK" face and returned to my full client load. One day the wall of denial and anesthesia broke. All the losses and separations I had experienced in my life collapsed in on me in nightly dreams. I realized that I had never learned to say goodbye effectively.

Exploring the impact of loss in my life, I began to realize that I was inhibited by the feelings of guilt about not being complete with the person that died. I had not been given or had not taken that last opportunity to say "goodbye" and "I love you." Never wanting to feel that immobilizing fear and guilt again, I began to explore messages that would allow me to be complete with everyone in my life. Promising to live my life consistently with these messages in every relationship, I discovered a new level of freedom and intimacy.

Messages for Completion

I love you. It may take some healing and communicating to get to the "I love you." Often a message of forgiveness about something that occurred in the past is necessary to uncover the presence of caring. The truth is that if we didn't care so much about this person, their leaving would not matter so much. Let people know on a daily basis what they mean to you. Acknowledge them for how much they mean to you and how much you value their presence in your life. Allow the tears to flow if that is what you feel. Many people say that if they shed any tears in front of the person leaving, it will burden them too much. Ask yourself this question, "Would you want to leave those you love and have no one shed a single tear? Would you think that you mattered to them?" Communicate the mattering of people in your life. Be vulnerable to the separation and the pain that it brings.

This is what you mean to me. These are the gifts and lessons we have given each other.

The significance of this person in your life brought many opportunities for upsets and pleasures, revelations and blockages. In acknowledging both, the relationship gains depth and meaning. Seeing both the positive and the negative in the context of lessons and gifts provides a depth and meaningfulness to the relationship.

It had a purpose, perhaps greater than you had realized previously. When we begin to communicate the contributions that people make in our lives every day, we begin to experience a sense of freedom and unrestricted intimacy. When we acknowledge others for what they mean to us, they are likely to respond in kind, telling us about how they value us in their lives. Sometimes the contributions are painful and frustrating; sometimes they are humorous. Share them all to the best of your ability. Even if the person you are completing with is deceased, the process of writing a letter or imagining a conversation with them is workable.

I am upset about losing you, and I promise to be whole and complete without you.

Acknowledge the complexity of your feelings and communicate the gift of wholeness that you are willing to provide to yourself and the other. Often when people are leaving or dying, they feel guilty and are unable to depart with ease because they sense the emotional trauma they are leaving behind. If you can declare your wholeness and bless the relationship and its journey, the opportunity for feeling and being complete is greater. The gift of completion eases the process of leaving and gives another permission to depart without the burden of causing undue damage to you.

While working with a woman who was newly diagnosed with acute leukemia, the doctor was surprised at the rapid physical decline in the patient. At first she was in severe pain. Soon afterwards she became severely disoriented and weak. Such a sudden decline was unfamiliar to the health professionals. I was called to evaluate the situation. When I directly asked the woman what was causing her to be so confused and to suffer so, she responded with lots of seeming gibberish and then said clearly, "My husband and son won't let me leave if I am fine." She was willing and ready to die, and subconsciously she was giving her family good reasons to allow her to let go. Her husband and son were extremely resistant to saying their goodbyes, to telling her that it was all right for her to no longer suffer and be free to leave. When finally they were able to share their love with her, the gifts of their relationship and the permission to go, the woman's mental condition cleared. She was able to acknowledge them and say her goodbyes. Within a few hours she had departed.

Forgiveness is a sacred Conscious Adult gift.

The forgiveness declaration: "I acknowledge that damage and harm was done to you and to me, and I now choose to release myself from the entanglement of the upset. I choose to be healed and to heal. To the best of my ability, I now promise to never use the incident or its story to harm you or me again in the future." Forgiveness that is chosen as a sacred gift lives as a declaration of soul and spirit. Such forgiveness can only be given by a Conscious Adult.

The Child may say, "I'm sorry." We even require it of them — but that does not mean that the Child can authentically gift forgiveness. The Child is focusing on making sure that safety is affirmed and that the love and relationship are intact. When the Adolescent says, "Sorry," the apology is often without real meaning. The teen is fulfilling an expectation in order to save face or maintaining an important relationship that it is unwilling to lose.

The process of forgiveness requires that we become conscious about the impact of the damage that has been done and that we make a conscious choice about healing or continuing the pain and damage. Authentic giving comes from first having given the gift of gentle compassion and forgiveness to ourselves. Without the gift of forgiveness, we get entangled in the synthetic web of guilt that imprisons our spirit and freedom of expression. If we validate our anger, pain, humiliation and shame, the opportunity to expand our joy and passion emerges. If we are unable to acknowledge our own participation in the upset, we project blame and cause on another. In certain situations, we may never be able to forgive the damage, but if we can begin to recognize what might have motivated the behavior of the person that caused our pain, we can begin to heal.

The Child has a right to be safe without being emotionally or physically abused. Abusive behavior that damages a young Child or Adolescent may never be forgiven but healing can begin if, in some small way, we can acknowledge the painful shame that an abuser must be living with. Even though it is not rational, the Child is left feeling responsible for having allowed or caused the abuse. The Child continues to ask, "Why did this happen? What did I do wrong?" The Child often concludes that something is wrong with it and therefore, it deserved the pain and shame. If, in meditation and with intention, we are able to give back the shame and pain to the abuser, to refuse to carry it any further as our own, the healing expands. If we carry unhealed shame and pain, it will seep out and be projected onto others, thus causing hurt again.

Forgiveness may be a process that occurs over time or it can happen in a single moment of sacred declaration. Forgiving at whatever level we can is crucial. With the intention to be healed, we may grant forgiveness to ourselves for having allowed an incident of pain and shame to occur, as well as to another who brought on the damage. When we are able to forgive, a profound shift in how we relate to ourselves and others occurs. The challenge to forgive another for the damage and pain they brought to us is often difficult. The Conscious Adult recognizes that without forgiveness, energy remains attached to the incident and the person involved in the upset. That energy is unavailable for creating and healing. Forgiveness opens the freedom of conscious choice, choice that is beyond the mundane.

Continue to dream and envision new futures, possibilities and commitments for yourself and others.

A dream without a commitment to action is nothing more than a good idea: a possibility without a probability of fulfillment. As we design our visions, consciously commit to living consistently with our promises and bring our dreams to reality, we begin to perceive ourselves as competent and successful. The future vision begins to design the present reality. The dream creates a resonance for the vision becoming real. As we live in that dream, an energetic receptacle is formed in which the dream can be collected and realized.

If we continue to hold onto our past as that which determines the future, so it shall be. The past-generated reality is predictable and looks very similar to how the past has always been. We have all changed our residence, our relationship and our jobs to satisfy our desire for change. Soon we begin to notice that wherever we go, there we are, taking our patterns and beliefs with us. We may change the external form, but the essence of creation lives in the beliefs of the past unless we consciously alter them. There is little risk when living from the past. We get to be right about how it is and always will be. The future-generated reality opens never-before known possibilities. There is great risk of living from a future design. We risk our egos, our vulnerability and our self-image. We risk failure, not achieving the goal we set out to accomplish. However, as a result of taking the risk, we introduce wondrous possibilities for ourselves and humanity. That which is outside the predictable, ordinary and perceived norm begins to happen more frequently, and we may begin to acknowledge, expect and trust in miracles.

Left to our normal patterns of thinking, self-defeating and disempowering conversations may frequently have us fall into the sludge traps of our negativity. Creating tools for reminding us to envision our dreams and to collect our miracles is especially important when we are designing new patterns of thinking and behaving. Posters, pictures and inspirational sayings, readings and audio programs provide stimulation for our targeted goals and dreams. As we think, speak and behave consistently with our best self, we create the resonance for an optimal reality to occur around us. Collecting miracles and things we are grateful for disallows the energy of martyr and suffering. We are left with a resonance of joy, love and trust that allows and perceives miracles more readily.

To get there requires living consistently with the qualities of being there.

The old phrases and beliefs continue to run our programs of reality whether we acknowledge them or not. It may help to first identify the scripts, beliefs and language that have defined our reality thus far, to claim the meaning of these patterns and their impact on our life, and then to identify a word or phrase that will lead us into a new reality that is consistent with what we say we want. As we design the future, it is important to identify the principles and behaviors that seem naturally present in that future vision. As we begin to live with those qualities in the present time, we engage in thinking, feeling and behaving as if the hoped-for future has already been achieved. As we live consistently with those qualities, we will begin to generate the resonance of that envisioned reality, thus increasing the probability of its becoming a sustaining energy in our lives. Soon we will be living more of that future vision in the now. It is important to continue to imagine new and inviting futures that have meaning and to always stretch for possible futures. Some say that if we can imagine it, it is possible. If we can imagine it and live the qualities of being in that future, we increase the probability of bringing the future into reality.

Choice is the key to living a life that is conscious, powerful and Adult. We have the power to create or react. How we respond to a situation is up to us.

If we live out of a feeling of victimization, we give others authority over us. We feel as though we have little or no choice. If we blame others for the conditions in our life, we project the cause of what happens onto some outside source. If we feel responsible for what is happening in our lives but that responsibility is felt as a burden and obligation, then the martyred suffering self will feel as though no other options are available. Living as victim or martyr will allow little or no choice, only reactions that automatically and repeatedly give the same response. If we acknowledge that responsibility provides us the power to make a difference, we are put in charge of our choices and our impact. Choosing with consciousness and responsibility requires the creation of an Adult being. The freedom to choose is only available when we are truly conscious.

If we never say "No," what is the power of our "Yes?" Practice the mantra: I shall not be "should upon" by myself or anyone else, and I shall not "should upon" anyone else.

If we never feel as though we have a choice and are caught in a caretaker role with others, we may feel the burdened responsibility of being all things to all people. Acknowledging the freedom to say "no," to behave differently than usual, is a healthy option. Weighed down with expectations and obligations, the imposed "shoulds" and "oughts" will stifle any possibility of freedom and authenticity. When we observe and stop the pattern of reaction, we are free to choose a response that is consistent with our valued principles and goals.

In researching my own patterns of feeling "should upon" by others, I began to see how I routinely perceived that people were making requests of me even when those requests were unspoken. Often, I would simply anticipate other's wants and provide for them without any invitation. It was as though I was reading their minds and knew what they didn't yet know for themselves. No wonder I felt exhausted with the burdened obligation I was placing on myself! My caretaking was so engulfing that others never even had the opportunity to make a request. Of course, I began to see that perhaps they never wanted or needed what I provided with such efficiency. I was left feeling martyred and unappreciated for my efforts and wondering why no one was providing in the same way for me. Of course, others never had a chance because I never gave them one. I was too independent and self-sufficient to ever lean on others. Besides, when others did attempt to help or support, they never did it good enough. Soon I realized that I "should upon" myself more than anyone else could and that I was the monster who was repeatedly generating this scenario of dissatisfaction and suffering. Learning how to wait for a request before moving into action, and giving myself the freedom to decline a request, was monumental in my rehabilitation. I began to realize that my caretaking was dishonoring of others' ability and potential. It was disempowering to others to perceive them as needing my intervention without their asking. Whether I realized it or liked it, I was communicating that I was better than they were. When I could recognize and admit the dishonoring in my behavior, the pattern began to lose power over my life. Trusting people and their own journeys expanded as a result. Being vulnerable and asking for what I wanted rather than waiting for someone to read my mind stretched my idea of what could happen in relationships.

The Adult by Choice designs life from a foundation of core principles and a clarity of purpose or vision. Living consistently with your principles will result in the designing of a strong character and identity.

People know you by your words and actions. Whether we realize it or not, each of us is motivated by core principles. These principles run deep and affect our perception and interaction in any situation with which we are involved. The core principles live as a perceptual grid through which everything in our lives is filtered and given meaning. When we are unaware of the principles and their impact, they live as obvious values that we presume everyone must have. We tend to run into difficulty when we interact with others to whom these values are not quite as important as they are to us. Often we hear ourselves make statements like, "Everyone knows that this is a problem. No one would ever think this is appropriate behavior. Everybody knows there is a right way to do things." Messages such as these might give us clues that a core principle is running beneath the conversation.

Exploring points of emotional upset can reveal important clues about your core principles. Upsets provide a clue about what really matters to you. Take an upset, especially a recurrent one, and examine it further. What do you see as the cause of the upset? What about the situation is intolerable for you? What are the common elements of this upset and others? What was your response in the situation? What is your justification and rationale for that response? In analyzing the incident further, explore the possibility that you might be upset as the result of an important value that matters a great deal to you.

While on vacation and walking through a marketplace, I saw a grandmother whipping a young boy about six years old. She held him by his upper arm high enough that his feet could not touch the ground. With some kind of switch, she repeatedly beat the child. He screamed and wailed. Without thinking, I blindly moved toward them to stop the beating. It was impulsive and immediate. I was stopped. I was being held in a full body grip. Finally I became aware that the man who had been showing me the marketplace was holding me with his massive arms, encircling me. It was impossible for me to move. Then I heard him pleading, "No, you mustn't."

I was so angry. The energy that poured through my veins had me struggling with a force that surprised me. When I finally gained my reason and realized what was happening, I was sobbing. "Why not?" I finally blurted out.

"Because if you intervene, he will get beat worse at home," he responded matter-of-factly.

I released my wild resistance and let go. My guide's arms cautiously released me and the tears rolled uncontrollably down my face as the intense energy that had driven me was released. The discussion that ensued revealed much about the culture, the patterns of discipline and the rights of elders over children. My own resistance to being dominated and spanked by parental figures was uncovered. My rage about any child being beaten and dominated by a grownup was exposed. When I heard that the child would be beaten worse if I tried to stop the beating by publicly embarrassing the woman, I was able to withdraw. I could not be a party to more beating and physical punishment.

A couple of years later, while grocery shopping with my son, I noticed coming down the aisle, an angelic, curly blond-headed two-year-old boy accompanied by a young woman and man who were engrossed with each other. Randomly, the tot touched some boxes of crackers as he hummed to himself. Suddenly, the woman grabbed the child, lifted him by his arm off the ground, and began beating him — her hand like a hummingbird's wings, an invisible flurry of hits to his small body. "I told you not to touch anything!" she screamed.

He did not cry or make a sound. It appeared as though he had stifled all emotion and had just removed himself from his body. "This is not the first time this has happened to him," I thought to myself.

As I passed by, I whispered with great intention, "Please stop!"

The woman's back was to me. Her furious hitting halted as suddenly as it had started. She turned and looked at me. "How dare you!" she blasted.

Noticing my son's blanched face and wide eyes, I told him to keep moving. As we turned the corner of the aisle, a wild animal jumped me from behind. My purse went flying. The insane fury was turned on me rather than on the young prey. My son stood in immobilized shock.

The police came, at first presuming that the grocery store incident had been an hysterical attack of two crazy women fighting over a watermelon. Finally they began to hear me…that I would do whatever it took to have a legal intervention in this home. When finally the police promised that Family and Children Services would be notified to come into the home and evaluate, I dropped the assault charges.

My son had been silent but clearly observing every detail. When we buckled our seatbelts in the car to go home, he looked pleadingly at me. "Promise me you'll never do that again."

"I can't promise that," I declared. "I cannot allow that violence in my world." I was stunned by my response. A sacred principle had voiced itself in the situation, and this time I had been able to make a difference.

Repetitive upsets can reveal that which is important to us. The current upset might remind us of a past hurt or wounding; it may also reveal that which is sacred to us, such as freedom: the freedom to speak, to express a point of view, to explore and design our own lives or to be safe. Identifying core principles can point to our destiny, to what makes our souls sing, and to our purpose for being.

Through the eyes of our principles, we design and assess our reality. We may have an affinity for many different principles and values, such as freedom, caring, compassion, integrity, serving, workability, self-expression, relationship, beauty and peace. However, some are more sacred to us than others. They grab our attention. They define a sense of satisfaction and determine our sense of mattering, of being at home with ourselves and our lives.

Picture yourself sitting on a three-legged footstool. Each leg of the stool represents a core life principle that governs your life. When all three core principles for life are rich and strong, your life will be in balance. If one is weak or another overused, you will be unbalanced and unstable. Much energy will be expended to stabilize the unsteady stool. Soon you may fall.

In researching my own principles, I noticed that I evaluated every situation from three perspectives: *integrity, service and workability.* Assessing the integrity of how something was done, the standards of performance and the quality of the product as well as the relationship of the people involved were very important to me. If something was integrous, it had also to be workable in the current situation or with the available resources. Something had to make sense, had to be possible and usually grounded in practicality. The idea that something would make a difference in people's lives and that it would serve them well was of equal importance. If the three principles were not in balance, I felt uneasy.

In understanding the power of these intrinsic values, it became evident that all three principles must be functioning and in balance concurrently in every situation. Each situation is automatically evaluated for the presence of integrity, service and workability in each aspect of the situation, the activities and the people involved. An action which may appear to support or empower one person might take away from or harm another. Thus, the action would be unacceptable for me. An idea may sound brilliant and enticing but be unworkable given current resources and conditions. If the action cannot be both of service without damage and be workable given the resources available, I am unable to validate its integrity. Unless all of the elements and principles are in balance at the same time, my personal alarm system begins to go off. The message is simple: "Something is not right here. This doesn't work. This is stupid. This may be pragmatic in the moment but is harmful in the long run."

In the past, when a situation felt off-kilter, I might have felt helpless to do anything about it, but went along with the program, not realizing exactly what was bothering me. I might have gotten frustrated and become positional and righteous about my position. Today, I have more freedom to choose to listen and respond to my internal whispers, to look through the valuing perspectives of my principles and to make distinctions that may be important not only to me but to others as well. I can then focus on what it would take to have the situation result in success for all who are involved. When my core principles function to support others, the values and insights can be appreciated and offered as gifts to others.

Defining Core Principles

Core principles are the key to expanding and expressing numerous values and distinctions for living a life that is satisfying and valuable. An artist or interior designer has hundreds of distinctions of color, form and texture. Passion and commitment direct the interest and research. So it is with core principles. The more we know about them, the more we want to know. The more we know, the more distinctions and options are available from which to make authentic and powerful choices.

Consider the word integrity. How would you define it? Included in your definition might be words such as honesty, authenticity, truth, communication and decision-making. The list could go on extensively, depending on the particular type of integrity being expressed and the particular passion that is being brought to the conversation. Each of those words might also be a core principle on its own. The distinctions grow as does the passion for continuing the research and exploration.

When we begin to live consistently with our principles in every domain of our lives, we begin to experience a sense of wholeness and peace. In my early thirties, I was impressed one day by a psychologist who presented a program about conflict resolution. In discussing the seminar with my professional cohorts, I was stunned by their invalidation of the man and the information in the seminar. "I don't trust a thing he says," spouted one person. "Don't you know anything about him? His family is a mess, and they are all taking drugs. His wife has attempted suicide many times."

The bottom line statement that left its mark with me was, "You know about people who go into psychology. They are just crazy and trying to fix the problems in their lives."

As I drove home, I wondered if that was what my coworkers thought about me since I was a "psych person." Would they think that my life was a mess? Would my family turn out to have serious problems? Would my four-year-old son become addicted to drugs? There certainly were no guarantees for success.

When I pulled into the driveway at home, I noted a sudden but perceptible shift in my energy. It was as though I had turned off the source of my public "alert and happy self" and had sunk into a tired weight of suffering. I watched myself take my things out of the car and enter the house. I saw myself mutter about the mess in the den and complain that nothing had been done to prepare anything for supper. My husband and son just stared and said nothing. Even though I was totally aware of my disturbing, martyred behavior, I was unable to stop it. It was obvious that if I continued to bring that private, burdened self to my family, the happy and participating family that I envisioned would never become a reality.

While I made dinner that night, I made a sacred promise that has been active ever since…that my public self and my private self would be the same, that I would bring my best self to my family, just as I did the public world. In fact, I hoped that I could bring more of my best self to my family and friends than the public world of opinion. The challenge is never-ending and each day requires a choice. My behavior and image in both worlds look more and more similar now.

In creating distinctions, we open the number of options available. When we increase the options, a sense of freedom emerges. When we make a conscious choice to take one or more of the options and close the door on others, we experience authentic freedom and authentic choice. In activating these choices, we also express an authentic authority and power in our lives, rather than experiencing a power by domination or manipulation.

The Child makes a decision. The Adolescent makes the decision a rule. The consciously choosing and committed Adult brings compassion to the research and reinterprets, heals and redesigns the decision as a core principle. The principles become the foundation for designing a conscious and satisfying life.

It is important that we start to identify our core principles, to research and develop them. We may then begin to see that a core principle opens the door to gifts, talents and unique individual mattering. Rather than being a righteous and dominating rule that often creates upsets and frustrations, the core principle can become a guiding light through the shadows of life. When claimed and placed in the hands of the Conscious Adult, the core principles bring a powerful peace and balance to life. When you consciously acknowledge and design your life from principles, passion is a natural by-product. When you live from your principles, your sense of character and identity emerges for everyone to experience.

Defining reality from a perspective of workability places personal responsibility at the helm and removes blame and projection from the equation.

Much of our daily conversations revolve around what we think, feel or opine about. We bolster our positions with justifying positions of information, expertise and experience. The result is a debate with dominating and submitting behaviors, and little is ever clarified or resolved. Exploring the workability of a situation provides specific distinctions for review and discussion. Communicating from a commitment to workability projects a sense of respect and productivity.

Conversations for Workability

No matter the situation, relating from a perspective of workability gives clarity and possibility to the conversation. Instead of describing what you like or don't like, what you are going to do or not do, practice the language of workability. As you become more masterful in speaking from workability, others will participate more freely and responsibly, sensing that they will be heard and respected. "This works for me. This does not work for me. This is missing for me. I envision these possible futures. I request and promise the following." This is the language of workability. Negative judgments and blaming are nonexistent in these conversations. As you practice using this language in every situation, communication becomes more objective and speaks only to what is true for you without judging what is important for someone else. The language of workability is a powerful language for the Conscious Adult.

What's Working?	What's Missing?
What's Not Working?	What Futures Are Possible? Requests and Promises

Summary

Designing and sustaining the Conscious Adult is a radical and refreshing journey of discovery and exploration. Recognizing the distinctions of the Child, Adolescent and Adult by Default as separate and unique from the Adult by Choice is imperative. Knowing the beliefs and concepts of the past that continue to invent the present if there is no intervention is necessary. Healing and reinterpreting the decisions made from fear, pain and shame from past experiences releases energy that may be directed toward developing new futures. Outlining dreams and visions for the future and becoming committed to the actions that are consistent with that future enhance the possible outcomes. Discovering your core life principles and living consistently with those values brings peace and satisfaction to life. The choice is always yours. To grow older is inevitable; to be a spiritual Conscious Adult is a choice. Choosing in every moment is required to have the Conscious Adult present. You are the only one who can choose.

Sylvia Sultenfuss

Ever-Expanding Distinctions

Having more distinctions creates more options, producing a sense of expanding freedom. When we make a conscious, authentic choice, we experience authentic freedom, which results in authentic power. When authentic power and choice are available, there is a natural desire for discovering and designing even more distinctions.

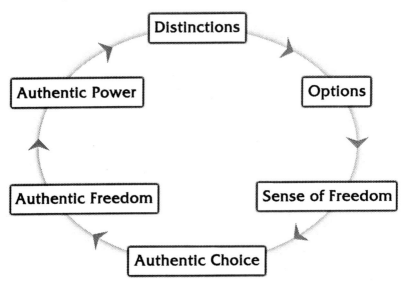

While teaching communication courses for health care professionals from all over the world, I had many opportunities to master the tools for discovering new distinctions. One day while working in a classroom of international students, we explored the power of a belief as a concept that, unchallenged, lives as fact in one's perception of reality. The students began to understand that new distinctions could alter perceptions, and therefore alter beliefs. I then pointed to someone's shirt and asked, "What color is this?" "Red," was the group's response. In my eyes the color was a shade of pink. I continued. "What is the color of this?" I pointed to something else. "Blue," was their response. I saw it as purple. Most were unable to see or identify colors beyond the primary colors found in a child's first box of crayons.

When I was able to assist them in seeing the shades of yellow or blue in the red or the blue and suggested alternative names for the color shades, most were able to see beyond the primary colors. Passing around samples of paint chips, the students saw new shades and names of colors, introducing many new distinctions. Opening the participants' perceptions for new discoveries, for new distinctions and for new colors in their crayon box, became a foundational tool in my teaching process. Once the participants realized the power of distinctions, I could return to that color discovery whenever there was resistance to opening new possibilities. When students became frustrated or stuck in a perception or belief that limited their ability to explore something new, I would remind them that they might be stuck in an old and limiting belief, one that was not necessarily wrong, just limited in perception. As a result, the process of expanding the learning was achieved with greater ease. Creating expanding distinctions is paramount in making effective and conscious choices.

Activities for Expanding the Conscious Adult Reality

Meditate and Visualize Positive Futures

Create a list of inspirational quotes and readings that stimulate a conversation that is positive and healing. There are many calendars and books that provide daily meditations to consider. Declare yourself in research about the meaning of the reading and allow the meditation to create a resonance and blessing in your life.

Predictably, the mind will generate plenty of self-defeating and fear-based thoughts. If we consciously bring readings, conversations and images that engage the best of our values and hopeful possibilities, we will continue to build the energy for creating new and positive futures. Let that inspirational reading guide you for the day or week. Explore its meaning and value for you. Let it matter to you. Allow it to alter your way of thinking and being.

Create Vision Posters

Vision posters are effective any time you want to focus your energy and attention to create a particular goal or vision.

Necessary items: Magazines, scissors, poster boards, glue sticks, colored markers, your personal marketing supplies and photos.

Collect a variety of magazines. Doctors' offices, salons and magazine recycling centers are wonderful places to find a good selection of magazines. If you invite others to make vision posters with you, ask that they bring magazines too.

Initiate the process with a short, eyes-closed visualization of what you want to let go of and what you want to bring into your life. Ask for guidance and assistance from your spiritual resources; they can create beyond your imagination.

Then begin to review magazines and pull out pages that have words, pictures, symbols and colors that draw your attention. Keep a steady pace as you rip out the pages so that your rational mind is kept at bay while your emotional, creative mind is allowed to flow. Don't question your choices. Allow any possibility to reveal itself. Give yourself freedom to color outside the lines. You may choose to use special art scissors that cut in unusual patterns. Use the front and back of the poster if you want. Let go of all the rules for how the poster should look.

To add focus and power, put your own business and marketing tools, including your name, on the collage. Photos of your face or those of loved ones can be included as a part of your visioning. Paste and write as many distinctions that add power and clarity to your visioning as you see fit.

Set a time limit for completing the steps to poster making:
Ripping and tearing: One half to one hour.
Cutting and trimming the items: One hour.
Gluing items on poster board: One half hour.
Final poster presentations: As long as it takes for everyone to share their vision with fellow participants.

(Without time limits, people often begin to lose focus, get lost reading articles or become dissatisfied with the items they have torn out for the poster.)

If there is a group making vision posters, establish a time for completion when each will present an individual collage. During the presentations, encourage everyone to share feelings and goals. Speak to the synergy that occurs when many align together to design visions.

Complete the process with a short meditation envisioning all of the goals and visions being achieved. Imagine living in that reality. Thank your spiritual friends for engaging with you in designing new futures.

Have fun and celebrate. Hang the poster in a place that you will see every day. The subconscious mind will begin to live with the visions and bring in the resonance of the poster. The power of advertising as it connects to and influences the subliminal mind is well-documented. The more that the mind sees the visuals, even when it is not consciously engaged, the more subliminal messaging and power the picture has.

Collect the Miracles

Write at least three miracles a day. Many people have to first identify what they are willing to call a miracle. Start writing whatever is comfortable at first. Then allow yourself to stretch the meaning beyond the beginning limits as you envision and call forth changes in your life and in the world. Before you go to sleep at night, review your day and collect the miracles.

The more you can acknowledge your participation in miracles, the more there will be a sense of personal choice and authentic power.

You may begin to realize your role in co-creating with your spiritual friends, with the Divine. As you claim the miracles in your life, the resonance of the miraculous, the-out-of-the-ordinary and the unpredictable will expand. You may begin the process by asking for and visualizing something small and immediate, like a good parking spot, and move on to sensing a personal impact in world affairs.

Participating in miracle work engages a relationship with others and with the Divine. Some people call it prayer, some call it intention, some gratitude. Expanding the energy of allowing the unusual enhances a sense of actively being a part of the spiritual dimension. It reminds you that you are a spiritual being on a human journey.

Identify Your Core Principles

1. Identify and list the conversations, upsets and issues that have your attention in life.
2. Identify the most frequent patterns or repetitive conversations.
3. Choose the three most repetitive conversation patterns.
4. Redefine and reinterpret these conversation patterns from rules and judgments to core principles from which you can design your life.

Answer the following questions:

1. What is it that drives you?
2. What frequently motivates your decisions?
3. What matters most to you?
4. When, historically, did you make a similar decision about yourself, someone or something else?

Once you define your core principles, identify what you are willing to do or not do to make them real in your life. As a result, you will define your character and identity. Others will know and describe you accordingly.

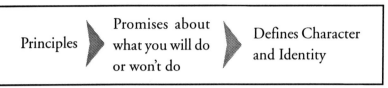

When you design your life from principles, passion is a by-product.

1. Make a conscious choice and commitment to living a principled life.
2. Add a commitment to bring to your exploration compassion for your own vulnerability and humanity.
3. Commit to being in research and design of your principles for the rest of your life.
4. From the compassion will come the passion.

Life Survey

Review the history of your life. Write out stories and incidents that you remember about your life at various ages. Especially focus on the decisions you made about yourself, others and life, such as success, having, receiving, trusting, loving, spirituality, self-expression and money.

Especially explore the wounding incidents in which the pain and shame were so great that the mind protected you by providing an anesthetic protection or amnesia. Many people say that they cannot remember a thing about their childhood before a certain age. As you begin to explore and become more trustable in being able to observe and experience your history without reengaging the horror of the incidents, the subconscious will reveal even more information and give more opportunities for healing and redesigning your life.

Identify and Explore Your Adolescent Wounding

Explore your adolescent wounding by identifying an incident, upset and painful event in which you experienced an important break in trust from those significant to you, especially those you hoped would love and protect you. Reveal your responses to the event by the promises you made about how it would be/would not be when you grew up. Notice the decisions and beliefs that were solidified in adolescence. This was a time of spiritual wounding that thrust you into the journey of exploring, discovering and redesigning your spiritual reality and relationships. It is from this research that the opportunity to choose and design an Adult by Choice occurs.

Writing/Re-writing Your Life Script

Write your life story on one page. Then shrink the page into one paragraph, then one sentence and then one word that defines a basic declaration from which you have lived your life. Meditate on that word and its impact in your life. Allow yourself to begin to see how your life reveals the evidence that this declaration has been real and valid. (You may use this process as you explore any domain of your life.)

Then write one word that you would like to be the foundation of a new and consciously chosen life. Then write one sentence that describes your new life, then one paragraph and then one page. For example, you may reveal the final word of your life script as fearful and choose the new script to be designed from a declaration of freedom.

Again, meditate on what your life could be and would be if you lived your life out of the new declaration. Look retrospectively at your life and collect any evidence for times when this declaration was already present and alive. Begin to expand that vision. Now see this new declaration expressing itself fully in your life. Bring it increasingly into your reality.

As you spend more and more time imagining the new declaration and its influence in your current life, you will build the resonance and energy for having that life be realized. Every day, collect evidence of the new script coming to fruition and flourishing.

Design a Research Project for Yourself Every Day

Identify questions that will challenge your current reality and beliefs. Give yourself permission to not know and just speculate and allow the possibilities to flow. Some say that at the time the child enters formal education, the ability to live in the question begins to diminish; that by the time one is a first year student in college, the freedom to not know has been significantly stifled. It is difficult to engage grownups in conversations for possibilities for longer than ten minutes before they start finding reasons that reject the posed possibility or before they begin to move into action.

Master the asking of powerful questions, those that open up many possible alternatives without a single specific answer. Allow all the ideas to be possible. Write about the discoveries and beliefs that limit your engagement in the creative process.

Suggested research questions:

1. What percentage of my day did I live in my Conscious Adult by Choice?

2. What percentage of my day did I not live in my Conscious Adult by Choice?
3. What am I making too real or not real enough?
4. If I lived out of the magnificence of my soul, what would happen in my reality?
5. What does it mean to live with integrity in every domain of my life? How do I expand it?
6. What is the meaning of love, money, relationship, intimacy, family, spirituality and friendship? How do I relate to these concepts in my life and in the way I express myself?
7. How can I bring the gift of forgiveness and completion into my relationships, with myself, with others?

Explore Situations from a Workability Perspective

Practice evaluating any situation as being workable or not for you. Practice describing what works for you or what does not. Eliminate the negative personal judgments and descriptions that define the situation as a problem, issue or concern. Continue to claim your own perspective without dominating anyone else with it. Experience the expanding respect and clarity that begins to emerge with the language of workability.

What's Working?	What's Missing?
What's Not Working?	What Futures Are Possible? Requests and Promises

Practice Forgiveness and Completion

Make a list of people with whom you are feeling incomplete or upset. Begin the process of healing and forgiveness.

Use the following form to identify what happened, your feelings about what happened and the stories, interpretations and decisions you made about what happened. Then identify specific actions that would heal or at least open up the communication blocks that now exist between you and another. Be honest with yourself about whether you are truly willing to forgive and be forgiven for the damage that was done.

Practice the forgiveness declaration that only the Adult by Choice can authentically make.

"I acknowledge that harm was done to you and to me. I cannot change what happened in the past. I now forgive myself and you. To the best of my ability, I promise to never use this situation, its history and the harm it caused against you or me again."

Practice the declarations of completion that open the doors of healing and letting go.

"I love you. This is what you mean to me. I am upset about losing you, and I promise to be whole and complete without you."

What happened/Facts Observable facts	Your Feelings Body sensations
Interpretations Stories/Decisions	Actions for Healing Declarations of Forgiveness

Sylvia Sultenfuss

Closing Thoughts

Practice is never done. Giving yourself research homework that will continue to expand mastery and clarity is imperative. Sustaining consciousness is a choice at every moment. It can never be taken for granted. The Conscious Adult by Choice can not and does not exist unless you say so.

The challenge is clear. It is now yours. Go into the world and make the Conscious Adult by Choice a reality in your life.

The Joy of Adulthood:

A Crash Course in Designing the Life You Want

is the first in a series of transformational books by Sylvia Sultenfuss.

For Additional Information:
Email: Sylvia@TheJoyofAdulthood.com
Website: www.TheJoyofAdulthood.com

Printed in the United States
21446LVS00002B/31-96